HIDDEN HISTORY
of
BANGOR

HIDDEN HISTORY

of

BANGOR

From Lumbering Days to the
Progressive Era

Wayne E. Reilly

THE
History
PRESS

Published by The History Press
Charleston, SC 29403
www.historypress.net

Copyright © 2013 by Wayne E. Reilly
All rights reserved

Front cover: Downtown Bangor before the fire of 1911. *Courtesy of Richard R. Shaw.*

First published 2013

ISBN 978-1-5402-2149-0

Library of Congress Cataloging-in-Publication Data

Reilly, Wayne E., 1945-
Hidden history of Bangor : from lumbering days to the progressive era /
Wayne Reilly.
pages cm. -- (Hidden history)
Includes bibliographical references.
Summary: "Forgotten stories and moments from Bangor's past"--
Provided by publisher.
ISBN 978-1-62619-010-8 (pbk.)
1. Bangor (Me.)--History--Anecdotes. 2. Bangor (Me.)--Social life and
customs--Anecdotes. 3. Bangor (Me.)--Biography--Anecdotes. I. Title.
F29.B2R455 2013
974.1'3--dc23
2013021769

To Madeleine, Benjamin, Alexander, Nora and Amelia

CONTENTS

Introduction   9

1. TECHNOLOGY TRIUMPHED
From Sails to Trains: The Decline of Bangor Harbor   13
The Rise of the Automobile   16
Bangoreans Couldn't Wait for the Wireless   19
Promise of Electricity   21
The Great White Flyers   24
The Kenduskeag Stream Transformed   28
First Airplane Flight Over Bangor   30

2. FROM STAGE TO SCREEN: THE BIJOU AND OTHER THEATERS
Norombega Hall Featured Presidents and Other Great Actors   35
The Opera House and the Auditorium   37
Going to the Movies: The Nickel and the Gem   40
The Queen City's First Vaudeville House   43
The Bijou: Bangor's Finest Theater   46

3. DISASTERS, TRAGEDIES AND MAYHEM
Six Bangor Boys Died in Sailing Accident   51
Murder at Aunt Hat's?   54
Bangor's First Auto Fatality   57
Cop Killer   60
"Gamble with Death" Caused Train Wreck   63

CONTENTS

Killer Heat Wave   65
Gas Explosion Rocked City   69

4. THE GREAT FIRE OF 1911
Small Fires Plagued City   73
Legends of the Great Fire   76
City Fought to Restore Utilities   80
"Strong Men" Seized the Day   84
Shack Stores Grew Like Mushrooms   87
City Swapped Park for New Post Office   90
Trade Triumphed   93

5. WHEN BANGOR LAUGHED
The Great Porcupine War   99
April Fools   102
Bangor High Boys Ran Riot   104
Escape of Eugene, the Mayor's Pig   107
When the Reverend Berry Did the Hoochee-Coochee   109
Bull vs. Auto   112

6. THE LIQUOR WAR
Liquor War On Again in Bangor   115
Rotten Bangor: When Carry Nation Stormed the Queen City   118
Judge Chapman's Impeachment   121
Judge Chapman's Revenge   123
Sturgis Men Invade   126
Liquor Amendment Survives Referendum, But Not in Bangor   128
"Our City—Its Pride and Shame"   131

7. THE PROGRESSIVE ERA
Three Bangor Reformers   135
Charities Sought to Help Woodsmen   138
First Public Playground   141
School for Immigrants   143
Voters' League Demanded Moral Reform   146
Boy Scouts' First Hike   149
There Will Never Be Another Jennie Johnson   152

Selected Bibliography   155
About the Author   159

INTRODUCTION

When celebrity aviator Harry Atwood made the first airplane flight over Bangor on June 17, 1912, local observers were ecstatic. Over the past few decades, they had witnessed men take to the air in balloons and dirigibles, but they had never seen a heavier-than-air craft get off the ground more than a few feet. Atwood's performances signaled the future. Flight would shorten the distance between the city, which seemed increasingly isolated far up on the Penobscot River near the very northeastern tip of the United States, and the major population centers along the East Coast and "Out West," where so many had moved in the past few decades. Optimists predicted Bangor would one day live up to its regal nickname, the Queen City of the East.

The local merchants who had sponsored Atwood's appearance wanted to let the rest of New England know that Bangor was back in business after the disastrous fire that had destroyed much of the downtown less than a year before. New buildings were going up, bigger and taller than the buildings that had burned. The city would soon have a new post office, high school, library and several churches, as well as hotels and office buildings. In the meantime, dozens of "shack stores" lined a few streets, as merchants attempted to get back on their feet.

Bangor was no longer known as "the lumber capital of the world." That honor had headed west along with many of the state's residents in the last few decades in search of more economic opportunities. That's why today you can see giant statues of Paul Bunyan from Bangor to California.

INTRODUCTION

Indeed, long before the great fire of 1911, the Queen City's busy harbor and lumber mills, its ice industry and shipbuilding business had all gone into decline. Efforts to open large textile mills and shoe factories had failed. Keen eyes had noticed, however, the growth of towns and small cities to the north and east thanks to the coming of the Bangor and Aroostook Railroad and the growth of the potato business and the paper industry. People in these hinterlands had always looked to Bangor for supplies. As these rural towns grew bigger, Bangor found itself evolving into the shopping center for the upper two-thirds of the state of Maine, stretching north, east and west away to the Canadian border, a place where people came for health care, advanced education and financial transactions, as well as groceries and hardware.

The historical essays in this book, my second volume of newspaper columns published by The History Press, focus on the part of this transitional period that lasted a little more than a decade, roughly between the time the first automobile chugged into town in 1900 to daredevil Harry Atwood's flying stunts. Vaudeville and the movies were taking over the theaters. The electric light bulb was still a wonder to behold, while the wireless promised a new world of communication. The train was the only way out of town in the winter when the harbor was frozen, and the Boston boats stayed out at sea.

Bangor was still "wide open" despite the fact that Maine had instituted the first-in-the-nation state prohibition law more than fifty years before. Lawmen half-heartedly battled the city's numerous saloons and brothels on an almost daily basis. This army of vice included Aunt Hat, the area's most notorious madam, who catered to the thousands of itinerant loggers and other workers who passed through the Queen City annually on their way to and from the North Woods.

At the same time, Progressive Era activists, a Christian army of ministers, professors, businessmen and clubwomen, sought to overhaul society. Reforms including night schools, playgrounds and children's clubs like the Boy Scouts were intended to help the poor, including the thousands of immigrants who had come to the city in search of work and a place to live. Nearly 40 percent of Bangor's population in 1910 consisted of immigrants or the offspring of immigrants from as far away as Russia and China. Even Carry Nation, one of the nation's most famous reformers, joined the fray, anointing the Queen City of the East with one more name—Rotten Bangor!

This book is divided into seven sections ranging in subject matter from technological triumphs to the fire of 1911 to Maine's first-in-the-nation prohibition law. Each section contains a half dozen or so of my columns published in the *Bangor Daily News* between 2003 and 2013. Each bears the original date of publication to make it clear what is meant in the text by "a century ago."

Back then, the city had two daily newspapers: the *Bangor Daily News*, which catered to Republican readers, and the *Bangor Daily Commercial*, a paper appealing to Democrats. I have spent ten years reading these newspapers week by week on microfilm searching for stories worth retelling. Most columns are based on months of newspaper stories as well as research in other sources, which are listed in the columns as well as in the bibliography at the end of this book.

Over the years, I have received a great deal of assistance from various individuals. I am especially obliged to Richard R. Shaw, whose books of historic Bangor photographs have done much to preserve the history of the city. Dick has been generous with information based on his extraordinary knowledge of his hometown. He has also provided me with most of the photographs and other images for my columns both in the newspaper and in my books.

Others who have been helpful include Bill Cook and Elizabeth Stevens in the Bangor Public Library's Local History Room, as well as several other librarians on the reference staff; Dana Lippitt at the Bangor Museum and History Center; the staffs in Special Collections at the University of Maine's Fogler Library and the microfilm reader room; Kevin Johnson at the Penobscot Marine Museum; and Jamie Kingman-Rice at the Maine Historical Society. A few other individuals and organizations are credited in specific columns. Special thanks as well go to the editorial staff at the *Bangor Daily News*, including my most recent editor, Aimee Thibodeau, and to Whitney Landis at The History Press.

Finally, my chief reader, librarian, critic and copy editor has been my wife, Karen, whose never-failing patience and interest made these columns possible. I would never have finished any of this without her encouragement and help.

Chapter 1

TECHNOLOGY TRIUMPHED

FROM SAILS TO TRAINS:
THE DECLINE OF BANGOR HARBOR

January 5, 2009

At the turn of the last century, Bangoreans worried about the declining traffic in their once fabled harbor. The "maze of masts" was no more. The rafts of logs and lumber that had once floated down the river one after the other from the sawmills between Old Town and Bangor were few and far between. The docks were run down and sometimes devoid of activity.

The subject of Bangor's decline as a port was pushed into prominence early in 1909 after it was discovered there had been a shocking drop in the amount of lumber shipped the year before. Bangor had always been about lumber and shipping. Were things as bad as they seemed to old salts hanging about the waterfront?

The *Bangor Daily News* offered a considerably more optimistic analysis of what was happening on January 9, 1909. The anonymous writer, a close observer of the city's riverine fortunes, got right to the point:

> It used to be said twenty-five and thirty years ago that when the lumber
> business should decline, Bangor would decline with it, and that the
> disappearance of the great fleets of old-fashioned coasters that used to
> crowd the upper harbor would mark the end of Bangor's importance as a
> seaport. Well, the lumber business, although in the aggregate for the state

Bangor's harbor, near the convergence of the Kenduskeag Stream and the Penobscot River, was a busy place during much of the nineteenth century. Railroad cars waited to load and unload cargo from the "maze of masts" that frequently crowded both sides of the river. *Courtesy of Richard R. Shaw.*

Opened in 1907, Bangor's new train station was a sure sign the city had become a railroad center while its harbor was in slow decline. *Courtesy of Richard R. Shaw.*

and for the Penobscot River region as great as ever it was, has undergone some remarkable changes, and shipments of the manufactured product from Bangor have declined to the lowest point since 1841, Bangor is in every way a larger and more prosperous city than ever it was before.

There were three principal causes for this economic shift, the writer explained. There had been "radical changes in the lumber business, including a great increase in the proportion of the product shipped by rail; a series of dull years in the lumber trade, and the diversion to Searsport and Stockton of business that had always been done here up to the time the Seaport division of the [Bangor and Aroostook Railroad] was opened to traffic [in 1905]."

Yes, things were changing, but they were getting better if you counted the number of new workers attracted to the city, the number of new buildings going up and the other indicators—even the number of new theaters—that showed capitalists had cash in their pockets despite the recent depression. To an old-timer, the mostly empty harbor didn't look right. To the visionary, who understood the dynamics of railroads, paper mills, waterpower, electricity and the other aspects of the new economy, profits were in the offing.

Maine continued to cut about 750 million feet of logs every winter, "but now-a-days, about one half...of these logs is manufactured into pulp and paper, instead of being sawed into boards and lumber," said the writer. "In that way we have big mills up north, and all along the rivers that afford good water power, and long trains of cars loaded with pulp and paper, instead of so many sawmills as formerly, sending millions of feet in lumber down in rafts to be loaded into waiting fleets of two-masted schooners."

He continued, "Evidently, there is more money to be made by turning spruce logs into white paper than in sawing them into boards. And, while Bangor has fewer schooners tied up off the City Point and off the Maine Central wharves, she has derived from the pulp and paper industry benefits which probably more than compensate for the loss of the coasting trade, or part of that trade."

The location of the mills had changed along with their function. The observer summed things up pithily: "In olden times, the log always came to the mill, whereas now the mill seeks the log." Once, dozens of lumber mills had been clustered between Old Town and Bangor. These sawmills had sent a constant stream of rafts of lumber down to the Bangor docks for shipment. Now there were only a half dozen or so of these mills along that stretch of river.

Other mills farther north in Aroostook County had once sent large amounts of lumber by train to Bangor for shipment by water. Now that lumber was bypassing the Bangor docks on the railroads. Meanwhile, the new Great Northern mill in Millinocket and other paper mills along the river were devouring logs that had once been sawed into lumber.

The report of the Surveyor General told the story. There had been a startling drop in the lumber business at Bangor's harbor in 1908 from the year before, at least in part because of the lingering recession. The shipment of dry pine, green pine, spruce and "hemlock, etc."—the four categories surveyed—had plunged dramatically. "When it is recalled that in 1872 there were surveyed at Bangor over 246,000,000 feet of lumber, the 92,000,000 of last year looks decidedly small," noted the writer, recalling the days when the Queen City had been described as the lumber capital of the world.

The city's coal trade was showing a similar trend. Before the opening of the B&A's Seaport line, nearly 400,000 tons of coal each season was discharged at Bangor by ship. In the last three years, that had declined to about 275,000 tons annually, the rest having been diverted to the new terminal at Mack Point in Searsport and shipped by train.

Foreign trade in the harbor showed a similar decline. Imported salt and exports of fruit-box shooks, clapboards, shingles and other products had all fallen off because of the railroads or other factors.

Today, the concerns about harbor shipping in the Queen City sound like a tempest in a teapot. Given the limited use of the river, even the expression "Bangor Harbor"—used so commonly in the newspapers a century ago—sounds odd. Ironically, the water is a lot cleaner and clear of debris today than it was then, as if the old harbor is waiting for a rebirth. What will replace the commerce that once enriched the city, however, is hard to tell—unless it is a riverfront museum dedicated to telling the exciting story of the "maze of masts" and the rafts of lumber that once floated by.

THE RISE OF THE AUTOMOBILE

April 20, 2009

When the actress Marie Doro announced in the fall of 1908 that she planned to arrive at the Bangor Opera House and other "one-night stands" in an automobile instead of on the train, it was one more sign that the horseless carriage was here to stay. "The idea is an entirely novel one," observed the *Bangor Daily News* on October 8.

In an editorial entitled "Motor Mania" appearing after the first Eastern Maine Automobile and Motor Show was held in Bangor a few months later, the newspaper declared, "The gasoline motor car is no longer

Bangor's first automobile show, held in the Bangor Auditorium in 1909, was a sign the new form of transportation was becoming popular in Eastern Maine. *Courtesy of Richard R. Shaw.*

an experiment. It has demonstrated its usefulness not only as a racing machine for millionaires and cranks to play with, but as a useful vehicle of travel, or for the delivery of packages and mail, for the carrying of passengers for pay, for the transportation of physicians…that it is now indispensable to modern civilization."

The first Eastern Maine Automobile and Motor Show, held at the Bangor Auditorium between April 19 and 24, 1909, a century ago this week, was perhaps the best evidence of all that the automobile was becoming indispensable to modern civilization as well as to auto dealers. By having one of these popular shows, the Queen City had clearly arrived.

Several Bangor dealers were represented. They included S.L. Crosby Company, agents for Overlands and Fords, G&J Tires and K.W. Magnetos; A.A. Robinson, agent for the Kissel Kar and Regals; L.A. Whitney, agent for Maxwells and Reos; J.H. Nash and Clarence Swan, agents for the E.M.F.; A.B. Purington, agent for Wintons; and Charles B. Treat, agent for Cadillacs. Salesmen arrived from Portland selling Knox, White, Franklin, Thomas, Chalmers-Detroit, Cushman and Lane Steamer automobiles that had been shipped ahead by train. In all, there were about thirty machines on the floor.

Big advertisements and booster stories by enthusiastic reporters, who most likely could not afford to own autos, began appearing in the city's two daily newspapers. The Portland Company in particular was anxious to tout its Knox. A large photograph in the *Bangor Daily News* showed eleven Knox Model-O cars worth $34,000 (in total) lined up on a residential street "just delivered to Portland customers." The Knox was "the greatest hill climber in Maine," according to a large display advertisement. The company had sold more Knox Model-Os in Portland that season "than all the other makes of the same approximate price put together."

S.L. Crosby wanted it known that its Fords could climb hills, too, and that its Overland was "NOT AN EXPERIMENT." They had been around, according to a large advertisement, "since the days of the bicycle," which wasn't actually all that long ago. The company produced the biggest display in the show—nine Overlands and Fords "profusely decorated with carnations."

By opening day, the cavernous auditorium at Main and Buck Streets, which also served as Bangor's opera temple or roller-skating rink or marathon track when circumstances demanded, had been attractively decorated. Hall's Orchestra was on hand to play marches, waltzes and overtures. But it snowed, and attendance was disappointing the first night.

Three display cars, all owned by distinguished local people, attracted the most attention, reported the *Bangor Daily News*. They were the Honorable Edward H. Blake's six-cylinder Overland, M.H. Andrews's Winton and Dr. Sawyer's four-cylinder Overland "finished in white." Innumerable exhibits had been set up displaying such accessories as tires, horns, lamps, speedometers and hand cleaner from the Flash Chemical Company.

As the days went by, attendance picked up. The B&A and the Maine Central Railroads offered reduced rates for attendees. Visitors from Old Town, Newport, Charleston, Belfast, Houlton and Caribou were among those on hand. Cadillacs were sold to people from Milo, Caribou, Brewer and Bangor. S.L. Crosby had sold seven Overlands and Fords. Every dealer sold at least one car, said promoters.

As the show continued, reporters were getting desperate for things to write about. Then they discovered one Mr. Dennison, a driver for the Knox Company who had raced for the Vanderbilt Cup. He would be participating in hill climbing and speed contests on Long Island in a few days. He had recently driven a mile in forty-seven seconds, "and that's going almost fast enough to satisfy most people," observed the reporter. "Twice he has been under the car in accidents, but his most serious injury has been broken ribs."

The evening of April 23 was ladies' night, when any lady accompanied by an escort would be admitted free. In fact, some ladies already owned their own autos, and many had been there buying "supplies," but tonight they would get special attention from the agents, and "the new gowns of the women will add much to the beauty of the already handsome decorations," declared the *Bangor Daily News*.

The show ended in another storm. Few braved the blast. Some, however, like Walter Savage, who made a last-minute purchase of a thirty-eight-horsepower purple Knox touring car he had been admiring all week, could no longer contain their motor mania.

The first annual Bangor auto show was declared a success even by a representative of the national magazine *Motor*. Next year's show had already been scheduled, and much of the space had been rented. As of June 7, fewer than four thousand autos had been registered in Maine, according to the *Bangor Daily News*. Imagine what would occur when Henry Ford got his assembly line up and running.

BANGOREANS COULDN'T WAIT FOR THE WIRELESS

December 14, 2009

"BANGOR WILL HAVE WIRELESS," declared a jubilant headline in the *Bangor Daily News* on March 8, 1906. In an era of miraculous technology that included light bulbs, movies and automobiles, the Queen City of the East was about to obtain yet another wonder confirming its status on the cusp of progress.

The wireless referred to wireless telegraphy, or radiotelegraphy—coded messages sent through the air without benefit of wires. The technology had been around for a few years, but it was still far from perfected or commercially available to everyone. Audio transmission, or what we think of as radio broadcasting, was still more than a decade away, although it had been accomplished experimentally.

"Bangor will have a wireless telegraph station in the near future," declared the *Bangor Daily News*. "J.S.B. Heath, manager for Northern Maine of the American DeForest Wireless Telegraph Co., is in Bangor, where he will remain until preparations are made for the installation of the station." Dr. Lee DeForest was the tireless inventor, who, it would turn out, was better at science than business.

A month later, on April 6, the newspaper carried another tantalizing bit of information. Another representative of the American DeForest Wireless

Telegraph Co. announced at a lecture in Bangor that the Maine Central Railroad had asked for a price quote on wireless telegraph service at Bangor, Waterville and Portland. When it was installed, people would be able to send messages from moving trains. Demand for the company's product was so great, however, that probably nothing could be done for the railroad for three years, said the report.

It would be nearly three years before more local stories about wireless telegraphy appeared in Bangor newspapers. On February 1, 1909, the *Bangor Daily News* announced that the steamers *Camden* and *Belfast*, which ran between Bangor and Boston, would be equipped with wireless outfits when they arrived in Bangor that spring. The president of the Eastern Steamship Company said that every passenger steamer should be equipped with a wireless rig. The benefits had been demonstrated during the last hours of the British ship RMS *Republic* off Nantucket in January. The *Republic* made history when it became the first ship to send a wireless distress message, after it collided with the Italian liner SS *Florida*. Hundreds of passengers were removed to safety by the ships that responded.

For the time being, however, the Queen City would have to wait for its own wireless. In Bangor, the word "wireless" had become a joke referring to the informal communication system used to alert saloon owners that the cops were coming. "The Wireless," an expression used in many newspaper stories about police raids, consisted of spotters stationed on roofs and street corners assuring that most saloons would be closed or dry when police officers arrived.

Things were progressing on the real wireless front, however. Amateurs were stepping into the breach. On March 30, the *Bangor Daily News* carried a photograph and a story about Howard Heath of Belfast. The sixteen-year-old high school student had set up his own wireless telegraphy station. He was receiving messages over a distance of a quarter of a mile. He had built a station at his home on Spring Street and another at the home of Roy Macomber on Bay View. Heath's feat was indicative of the vast number of similar efforts going on as inquisitive tinkerers read excitedly about the accomplishments of men like Guglielmo Marconi and Lee DeForest.

Just three weeks later, both Bangor newspapers reprinted a story from a Jacksonville, Florida newspaper, indicating once again that Bangor was about to have a wireless station. The Queen City was on a long list of communities where the Atlantic Radio Co., which was then handling "the DeForest wireless telephone system," was planning to locate towers from Eastport, Maine to Texas. Once again, it was stated, the company had an office in Bangor with a district manager.

Then came a great surprise. A century ago this fall, on November 29, the Bangor newspapers acknowledged the city already had a wireless station (well, almost) and had received its first complete wireless message. The owner was not a famous scientist or a business executive. He was a tinkerer, an "amateur electrician" and an employee of the local phone company. "While a number of amateur electricians in and around Bangor have been experimenting with wireless telegraphy for some time, as far as known the first complete message picked up by an outfit here was read by Frederick Rogers of 24 Sixth Street on Saturday night when he heard the station in the Waldorf-Astoria Hotel in New York send a message to Chicago. Mr. Rogers has also picked up messages from the Marconi station on Cape Cod reporting shipping news and fragments of messages from other stations," reported the *Bangor Daily News* that morning.

Rogers, with "material assistance" from P.J. Bell, "toll wire chief of the local exchange and an expert electrician," had constructed the station using a receiver made by an electric supply company and an aerial consisting of wires running from a seventy-five-foot pole in his yard to a pole on his house the same height from the ground. He was planning soon to set up a transmitter, which, according to the *Bangor Daily Commercial* that afternoon, would be Bangor's first wireless telegraph station "of any capacity."

In fact, the *Commercial* added, two young men on lower Main Street had stations that enabled them to send messages to each other and catch snatches of signals passing overhead to ships at sea. And "two boys in Brewer have similar stations, it is understood."

Imagine the excitement generated then by these feats of technological prowess! I remember as a boy receiving a little do-it-yourself crystal radio set for Christmas and casting it aside in favor of my own transistorized version. Progress was marching on. By then, the awe inspired by the first wireless transmissions received by tinkerers like Fred Rogers had been long forgotten as we waited for the Internet.

Promise of Electricity

February 7, 2011

Technological developments were transforming Bangor a century ago. Automobiles had begun coughing and sputtering along the streets a decade before. Movie theaters opened a few years later, and young tinkerers began

Merrill Trust Co. and a section of the "White Way," stretching from Exchange Street to Bangor's old City Hall at Hammond and Columbia Streets, as they appeared lit up for the city's Food Fair and Winter Carnival in 1913. *Courtesy of Richard R. Shaw.*

experimenting with wireless receivers about the same time. A dirigible had floated over the Eastern Maine State Fair, and before too long, an airplane would buzz over the Queen City of the East.

The family household was one place where the average person could experience some of the most noteworthy high-tech transformations—electrical gadgets that made life easier. All you had to do was have the money to hook up to the expanding electrical grid and then pay the electric bills later.

The best place in Bangor to get an idea of what was available, electrically speaking, in February 1911 was the Winter Carnival and Food Fair held at City Hall, then located just up from West Market Square at the corner of Hammond and Columbia Streets. Hundreds of people attended from as far away as Aroostook County.

The Bangor Railway and Electric Company's exhibit, "The Electric Home," was one of the most popular attractions. The company had been laying down tracks and power lines for some years as the trolley system expanded. If residents wanted, the company also wired homes along the new trolley routes. Eventually, the trolleys stopped running, but by then, the Bangor Railway and Electric Company had evolved into the Bangor Hydroelectric Company.

"The Electric Home" display of 1911 consisted of three rooms—a kitchen, dining room and bedroom—with the latest electrical amenities. The kitchen contained "an electric range, a fireless cooker, ice cream freezer, flat iron, washing machine, hot water urn and waffle liner," according to the *Bangor Daily News* on February 8. It was necessary to add the phrase "all these utensils being operated by electricity" in case some country fellow still didn't get it. The dining room contained a similar array of electrified wonders: "a chafing dish, bread toaster, coffee percolator, vacuum cleaner and tea pot." In the bedroom, the excited visitor could see an electric "bed lamp, heating pad, hair drier, luminous radiator, sewing machine and nursery milk warmer."

Two days later, the reporter revisited "The Electric Home," perhaps to satisfy the complaints of readers who feared electricity was too expensive, unsafe or unsightly. Some people feared electricity could jump out of power outlets and start fires. "In the planning of the electric lighting arrangements of the electric home at the Food Fair, careful attention has been given to secure efficient illumination in an artistic manner without losing sight of that important item ECONOMY," the reporter explained. The secret, he said, was Mazda lamps, a brand of incandescent light bulb. "These lamps are used in all positions, hanging pendant in the ceiling fixtures and standing upright in the wall fixtures," he noted.

These "arrangements" were described in minute detail for people who had perhaps only seen an electric light bulb in a newspaper advertisement or in a store:

> In the kitchen, one 60 watt Mazda lamp provides a splendid general illumination, while the dining room is equipped with a center dome in which are installed three 40 watt Mazda lamps; the object being to throw the light on the table without having the rays in the eyes of those seated about it.
>
> The [bed] chamber has a centre fixture for general illumination, with wall brackets on each side of the dresser or my lady's toilet. On the desk is a charming portable lamp, and attached to the head of the brass bed is a bed lamp for reading in bed. The lamps used in the chamber are 25 watt Mazda, and the illumination obtained is more than ample, the yellow wallpaper aiding the lighting greatly.

By the end of the Bangor Winter Carnival and Food Fair, the city definitely had decided that displays of electrical prowess in the streets were the way to impress visitors. City street lights were already electrically powered. For the carnival, however, lots more light bulbs were strung around the downtown, outlining buildings and illuminating sidewalks, in an effort to give the area a "metropolitan look." The dim, gaslit days when intoxicated loggers were mugged in the shadows for their winter's pay or walked off the docks at the end of dark alleys into the Kenduskeag Stream were about over.

"There is a decided sentiment…that the brilliant electrical illumination, or at least part of it, shall remain," reported the *Bangor Daily News* on February 10. "Bangor streets never looked as pretty, and it seems a pity say those who favor the illumination plan to have them revert to semi-darkness. The more metropolitan the streets, the more people seem to catch the true metropolitan spirit—the spirit of shopping and theater going. Electricity, as an incentive to sight-seeing, has a very definite and practical value."

The Winter Carnival and Food Fair lasted a week. Declared a success by its organizers, the United Commercial Travelers' Bangor Council, an organization of traveling salesmen, plans were already underway to hold it again in 1912, when there would be new and better-designed electrical gadgets. In such ways did Bangor emerge from its logging and maritime past into a new economy in which it became the shopping and cultural center of Eastern Maine.

THE GREAT WHITE FLYERS

June 15, 2009

"SWIFT TWIN TURBINERS FOR FAMOUS OLD BOSTON-BANGOR LINE," announced a large headline in the *Bangor Daily News* on June 14, 1909. "Camden and Belfast, Handsome Sister Ships of Steel, Succeed The Wooden Sidewheelers Next Week—Down East Steamboat History."

The Eastern Steamship Company was replacing its old side-wheelers the *City of Bangor* and the *City of Rockland* with two bigger, faster turbine-powered, propeller-driven, steel-hulled vessels. The change marked "another epoch in the history of a service famous for nearly a century," said the newspaper. Nothing much caused more excitement in Bangor, save the arrival of the circus, than the inauguration of a new Boston boat.

The steamer *Belfast* of the Eastern Steamship Company. *Courtesy of Richard R. Shaw.*

The Eastern Steamship Company's terminal on the riverfront in Bangor. *Courtesy of Richard R. Shaw.*

The sister ships were built at Bath Iron Works. They were the first Boston boats to boast steel hulls and turbine engines. The *Camden* had made the Bangor-to-Boston run two years ago for a few months but had been withdrawn because of handling difficulties at some of the route's smaller landings. Wharves had been straightened and expanded to accommodate bigger vessels, and now it was time to make the transition. The *Belfast* had been launched only recently. She was making her maiden voyage from Boston to Bangor on June 21.

During the summer, the boats left Boston at 5:00 p.m. on alternating days, making a direct run to Rockland and then stopping at Camden, Northport, Belfast, Searsport, Bucksport, Winterport and Bangor the next day. They left Bangor at 2:00 p.m., retracing the route.

The "Cities" weren't being mothballed. The *City of Rockland* was going to work on the St. John-to-Boston run, while the *City of Bangor* had been assigned to the Kennebec River.

Bangoreans were enthusiastic at the thought of new Boston boats, the latest baubles to decorate the majestic Penobscot and their little harbor. Naturally, a great deal of reminiscing was underway. "Steamboating down east is a different thing now from what it was in the old days," mused the *Bangor Daily News*. "It is related by old travelers that before the war, and even later, the bill of fare on the boats consisted chiefly of ham and eggs. There was nothing much to eat, but plenty to drink. Now there is a great variety to eat, and not so much drinking."

The 321-foot *Belfast* was a commodious luxury liner, as described by the *Bangor Daily News* on June 23. A large "social hall" furnished with mahogany armchairs was located on the main deck. Attached was a dining hall that would seat one hundred people at small tables instead of the "usual long tables" of yore. Furnishings and decorations "are in silver gray with a touch of gold." A women's social hall sat aft of the dining saloon, furnished in "rattan and plush." A similar room for men was located toward the bow. The *Belfast* had 186 staterooms on the saloon and gallery decks. There were also 102 berths in the men's cabin and 61 in the women's. The saloon and promenade decks afforded a traveler a most enjoyable opportunity to take the air once at sea.

In an age when average men were as interested in horsepower as they were in horses, the power source was described in exacting detail:

> The Belfast *is driven by turbine engines. There are three of these turbines, one receiving the high-pressure steam and the two others operating on the exhaust steam from the first. Each turbine drives its own separate propeller shaft with a five-foot phosphor bronze propeller, making 500 revolutions per minute. In all, the three turbines deliver 4,000 horsepower to the propellers. This power is generated in a battery of four great Scotch boilers,*

*the standard marine type for big ships. Each boiler is of over 1,000
horsepower and is fed through three furnaces, the ship therefore requiring in
all 12 furnaces to furnish power for her turbines and auxiliary machinery.*

"Gloom prophets" were already questioning a few things before the *Belfast*
set out on her maiden Bangor voyage. Not having taken any time trials
between various islands and other landmarks, how would the *Belfast* do if
she encountered heavy fog along the way? Would her big turbines be too
powerful for the delicate twists and turns in the river?

The newspapers answered with soothing reassurances: "This ship is the
delight of even the most timid passengers, for she possesses the same strength
of hull, the same ratio of power and the same elements of safety that are
possessed by trans-Atlantic liners." And in fact, "Quartermasters who
brought her through said she steered like a rowboat," reported the *Bangor
Daily News* after the *Belfast* navigated the river. Captain Ezra W. Curtis, who
had taken over the *Belfast* with his entire crew from the *City of Rockland*,
pronounced the run a success in every way.

The arrival of the *Belfast* in Bangor just after noon on July 22 was a scene
of noisy exuberance. Smaller boats blew their horns in salute, and the *Belfast*
saluted back. Mill whistles added to the din. Bands played on deck and on
shore. More than one thousand people cheered from the deck, large crowds
having gotten on at river ports beginning in Belfast. A cheering Bangor
crowd greeted them at the steamboat wharf.

By 2:00 p.m. the *Belfast* was ready for her return trip. A raft of logs floating
through the harbor held her up for fifteen minutes, reminding everyone that
the Queen City, once the "Lumber Capital of the World," was still fully
deserving of the best steamboats money could buy.

The next morning, the *Camden*, skippered by Captain Frank Brown,
arrived in Bangor, having passed the *Belfast* after midnight a short distance
to the westward of Monhegan headed for Boston. The rhythm of the Great
White Flyers, as the Boston boats were also known, had been established for
yet another summer.

The average viewer of that event a century ago would have been shocked
to learn that twenty-six years later, in 1935, the *Belfast* would make the last
voyage from Bangor to Boston for the Eastern Steamship Company, and
the Boston boats would pass into history, victims of competition from trains,
planes and automobiles.

THE KENDUSKEAG STREAM TRANSFORMED

December 13, 2010

Looking down the Kenduskeag Stream from the State Street Bridge toward the Penobscot River back when sailing ships were a common sight along the lower part of the stream. *Courtesy of Richard R. Shaw.*

The next time you take a stroll along the sidewalk next to the Kenduskeag Stream between State and Washington Streets, pause a moment to imagine the past. You are walking where thousands of sailing ships were once tied up, sometimes side by side, when this section of the Kenduskeag was much wider and located in the heart of Bangor's working waterfront. That stretch of the stream was triple the width it is today. My 1875 "Birds Eye View" map of Bangor shows nearly twenty schooners tied between State Street and the Maine Central Railroad drawbridge at the mouth of the stream. From what I have read, this is an accurate representation of activity there for much of the latter half of the nineteenth century, well before city fathers decided to tame the stream.

A century ago, navigation up into the stream was declining, just as it was along the river. "ONLY 99 SCHOONERS," reported the *Bangor Daily Commercial* sadly in a headline on November 26, 1910. "KENDUSKEAG UNPOPULAR, Fewer Vessels Entering the Stream As Year Succeeds Year."

F.H. Sylvester, the man assigned to open the drawbridge maintained by the railroad, reported that only 99 vessels had come through the bridge so far that year, and he didn't expect anymore. There had been 123 in 1907, 116 in 1908 and 118 in 1909. This was back in the days when both Bangor newspapers employed a shipping news reporter, and doings in Bangor Harbor symbolized the lifeblood of the city.

"Most of the schooners to enter the stream this summer, have, as usual, been small, although one or two good-sized three-masters came in out of the Penobscot, notably the *Margaret G.*, a Britisher bringing salt for Towle [J.N. Towle & Co., 82 Broad Street]. The *Jewell* has brought lime to Dunning [R.B.

Dunning & Co., 54 Broad Street], every trip, and sometimes sailed light and sometimes with lumber from H.F. Andrews [66 Exchange Street]. Other craft have also brought in lime," the reporter wrote. Not a yacht or steamer had sought admission that summer, nor had a scow or even a raft of logs demanded entry.

No accidents had been reported. Once, however, the main shaft had broken in the draw, and it was necessary to use a rope to move the bridge that day. Typically, the bridge was open for about five minutes but never more than seven, said the tender. It had been opened often at night, causing less inconvenience for pedestrians.

Of course, in those days, if you wanted to cross the stream in a wagon or an auto, you had to go up to the State Street Bridge. All that would change in 1930, when a new bridge would open between Broad and Washington Streets for growing motor traffic, but no draw would be included to admit stray sailing vessels. By the 1920s, shipping in the Kenduskeag had shrunk to almost nothing. It had gone from fifty-seven vessels in 1920 to ten in 1925, according to figures supplied by the Maine Central Railroad to the *Bangor Daily News* on October 12, 1925. Two years later, only three vessels appeared.

The debate over the bridge was being conducted in earnest by then. Should it include an expensive drawbridge mechanism? The *Bangor Daily News*, which had its offices on Exchange Street, was a diehard backer of a drawbridge, but even its old historian, quite possibly the famed editor Lawrence T. Smyth, who had worked for the city's harbor master as a boy, had a hard time convincing anyone.

"Time was when hundreds of vessels of all rigs and sizes, from a bay coaster to an 800-ton bark, came into the stream to discharge their cargoes, and when the late Gilbert Fickett, draw tender for many years, was kept busy every high water with the passage of shipping in and out," wrote the newspaper's maritime expert on December 21, 1927. "Recently, with the vanishing of the lumber trade and the practical monopoly of general cargo carrying by rail or steamer, the Kenduskeag shipping has fallen to almost nothing, and the wharves that were formerly busy places now are deserted or covered with extensions of the stores facing Broad and Exchange Streets." But, he continued, "no man knows what the future holds, what commercial developments there may be in years to come that may make free navigation to the city's heart as valuable a privilege as ever—or more so. It is not safe to assume that there never again will be any use for those wharves."

However, Franklin Bragg of N.H. Bragg, which had its offices on Broad Street, said his company was willing to take its chances without the draw. It would be expensive and might pose a hazard in the event firemen needed to get their equipment across the bridge when it was open. Bragg represented the majority. The compromise that resulted led to building a bridge that would allow installation of draw equipment if the need was seen later.

Of course, it never was. In his annual report in 1930, Harbor Master Edward Lord declared it looked as though the stream was permanently closed because of the new drawless bridge and because of the way the Maine Central had placed its rails across its own drawbridge at the mouth of the stream.

The new bridge connecting Broad to Washington was described as part of "the Atlantic highway" through Bangor, a mighty thoroughfare "accommodating traffic from the Bath and Rockland road to Lucerne, Bar Harbor, Washington County and the north." Nobody had heard of the interstate yet.

Another part of the plan was to build "two grand parkways" along the Kenduskeag between the new bridge and the State Street Bridge. The stream would be narrowed with retaining walls, and on its banks, behind the businesses, would be parking spaces and a public road on both sides. The "unsightly conditions of the rear of the storehouses" would be eliminated, and perhaps something could be done about the odor of sewage from the stream at low water in the summer.

At the time, the *Bangor Daily News* described this plan as "a bit fantastic... absurd, not to say dangerous...something for the lawyers to argue about. Has the city or anyone the right to substitute a street for tidewater?"

This vision, the Kenduskeag Plaza, was not completed until 1962 as an Urban Renewal appetizer. The stream was narrowed from 250 to 80 feet between the bridges on State and Washington Streets. The inner sidewalk marks where the old rotting wooden cribwork once held up the bank. The outer sidewalk marked where schooners had once unloaded their cargoes.

Watch your step the next time you walk along there. Don't fall into the open hatches or trip on the coiled lines. Listen for the creaking rigging and the shouts of the stevedores. And enjoy the view.

Thanks to John Frawley for some of the information in this column.

First Airplane Flight Over Bangor

June 11, 2012

The Bangor Street Fair and Carnival was held a century ago to celebrate the Queen City's recovery from the great fire that had devastated much of the downtown the year before. Bangor had seen plenty of circuses, carnivals and fairs over the years, but this one was going to be unique, "a sort of Mardi Gras carnival" lasting an entire week.

The Ferrari-Bostock Animal Shows and Circus spread its acts across the downtown, with a wild animal show in East Market Square, a musical comedy company in Haymarket Square, a "crystal maze" on State Street where the old Post Office in the Kenduskeag Stream had burned, a vaudeville tent on Central Street featuring a professional wrestler offering twenty-five dollars to anyone he couldn't throw in fifteen minutes and much more. The purpose, of course, was to encourage people to shop in the newly rebuilt stores.

Plenty of other diversions aimed to attract shoppers. Daily parades featured brass bands, decorated automobiles and fraternal organizations too numerous to mention. There were also five U.S. Navy torpedo boats with three hundred sailors tied up in the harbor. A ten-mile marathon was run between Orono and Bangor, while an uphill car race on Cedar Street's steep incline gave auto enthusiasts the opportunity to test the power of their engines.

Celebrity aviator Harry N. Atwood made the first airplane flight of any height or duration over Bangor as part of a carnival intended to demonstrate that the city had come back after the fire of 1911. *Courtesy of Richard R. Shaw.*

The biggest event by far at this "monster carnival," however, was the appearance of Harry N. Atwood, currently the nation's most famous aviator, the daredevil who would finally show Bangoreans what the twentieth century looked like as he soared over the city.

In 1912, flying machines were objects of awe that caused people to point to the heavens shouting in wonderment. A visit from Harry Atwood, a national hero, was just what Bangoreans needed to reassure them they had indeed made a successful comeback from the nightmare conflagration of the year before. His appearance was also a way to attract the crowds necessary to help merchants pay their debts.

"Why, just let them know throughout Eastern Maine that Harry Atwood will fly here, and so many people will pour into Bangor they'll have to camp in the streets," exclaimed an enthusiastic booster at a meeting of merchants at the Bangor House to discuss the likelihood of Atwood's appearance. Posters hung around the dining room said things like "Boost Bangor" and "No pessimists admitted."

Atwood arrived in Bangor in early May to sign a contract and discuss arrangements. He was described in the Bangor newspapers as "holder of the world's record for the longest one plane flight—from St. Louis to New York via Chicago using but one machine—and the longest hydro-aeroplane flight from Boston to Providence, RI...around the point of Cape Cod." Such records would soon be broken, and Harry's accomplishments would be forgotten as the years passed.

Atwood, twenty-seven, was described as clean cut, eyes "clear and straightforward" and with firm-set mouth "denoting determination and daring." In other words, he could be trusted. The last aeronaut to visit Bangor, C.C. Bonnette, had angered the crowd at the Eastern Maine State Fair when he failed to fly his airplane as promised. The day after the fair ended, he had managed to get his aircraft a few feet into the air but landed before leaving the fairgrounds.

Atwood reappeared in Bangor on May 23 at another "Boost Bangor" dinner for 150 local businessmen at the Bangor House. He gave a speech in which he reassured his audience that his flying was "safe and sane." Death was a frequent spectator at early aviation shows. Atwood had had several brushes with the grim reaper himself. He recounted the last moments of the life of St. Croix Johnstone, who made the first significant flight in Maine from Augusta up and down the Kennebec Valley on August 9, 1911. Atwood had been flying near Johnstone and another pilot when both were killed in an exhibition over Lake Michigan just a week later.

A few days after this Bangor speech, Atwood had "his latest close call" during an exhibition at Fitchburg, Massachusetts, when his plane dropped six hundred feet to the ground for a surprise landing when the engine died.

Towing his airplane behind his large touring auto, Atwood arrived in Bangor (along with his three "mechanicians") ready for business on Sunday, June 16, the day before the opening of the carnival. He was in the air by Monday evening, a day ahead of schedule. At 6:23 p.m., he took off from Maplewood Park (today's Bass Park) in his Burgess-Wright biplane, "and Bangor's first real aeroplane flight had begun," declared the *Bangor Daily News* the next morning.

No one was expecting the flight. "The news spread…by a sort of wireless," reported the newspaper writer. "The streets suddenly filled; so did windows and housetops. Thousands of eyes were strained to catch a glimpse of the big machine, which floated at an altitude of 1,000 feet like some graceful white-winged bird."

Atwood circled the city farm and then headed for the Thomas Hill Standpipe. A few moments later, he was over the pumping station at an altitude of 1,500 feet. Then he headed down river.

Pandemonium broke loose. Three hundred sailors flung their hats into the air, letting out a tremendous cheer as he passed over the navy boats. "Whistles of all the craft in the river and of the mills along the banks united in a terrific din." After circling South Orrington, Atwood returned to Maplewood Park. "No such flight was ever before attempted much less accomplished in Eastern Maine," declared the newspaper.

Atwood flew over the city several more times that week. He was indeed a hero, always polite and accommodating. When he was forced down early by "bad air currents" Tuesday evening, he promised to make more flights each day at the end of the week. When a young man was severely injured on his motorcycle at the hill-climbing race, Atwood insisted on taking him to the hospital in his auto. He also agreed to give a short talk at the Bijou Theater, describing his exploits in his usual entertaining but modest way. He decried "circus stunts" as a cause of many deaths among flyers, but on Thursday he performed a "dead-engine" spiral for his audience at Maplewood, causing gasps of awe.

Early Friday evening, he took off in his plane for another appearance at Poland Spring the next day, following the Maine Central tracks. As dusk fell, he was forced to land in a field in Pittsfield, instead of Waterville, his goal that night. This created a local sensation. Towns along his route had been tipped off by telegraph that he would be flying over.

"He came down near the Slipp crossing about a mile and a half west of the village and made such a sudden drop that word spread of a terrible calamity. This started a great rush of autos down the road. But the clever aviator had simply made an easy landing in Fred Drake's field," reported the *Bangor Daily News* on June 22.

The Bangor Street Fair and Carnival ended the next day. Miss Rosella Cassidy was crowned queen with 11,954 votes. P.M. Lawrence, driving a Chalmers 40, won the prize for the fastest time in the hill-climbing competition up Cedar Street. Harold Barton, a Bangor boy, won the ten-mile marathon between Orono and Bangor (probably because his stiffest competition, Andrew Sockalexis, the Penobscot Indian, was in Sweden competing in the Olympics).

Two of the city's major post-fire achievements almost got lost in the excitement—the laying of the cornerstones for a new Bangor High School and the Bangor Public Library next to each other on Harlow Street. But the one event that no one would ever forget was Harry N. Atwood soaring overhead. Finally, Bangoreans could say proudly they had seen a real airplane fly.

Chapter 2

FROM STAGE TO SCREEN: THE BIJOU AND OTHER THEATERS

NOROMBEGA HALL FEATURED PRESIDENTS AND OTHER GREAT ACTORS

October 20, 2003

On Friday morning, October 16, 1903, a crew of workmen began tearing out the stage on the second floor of one of Bangor's most famous buildings. The voices of President Ulysses S. Grant and the country's greatest actor, Edwin Booth, as well as a host of other ghostly dignitaries still rang out loud and clear through the dark recesses of Norombega Hall for the *Bangor Daily News* reporter sent to cover the nostalgic event.

The quiet park called Norumbega Parkway (yes, the spelling has been changed), where passersby can sit serenely soaking up the sun and reading a book today, was once the site of the massive Greek Revival building, constructed and elaborately decorated in 1855 on a granite platform in the Kenduskeag Stream between Central and Franklin Streets.

On the first floor were fourteen stalls where merchants sold their wares. That aspect of the building's past had gone out of business five years before.

On the second floor was the hall—117 feet long, 56 feet wide, with a 39-foot-high ceiling. One Bangorean booster had compared the building favorably to Boston's Quincy Market, but circumstances were changing in the Queen City. New, modern theaters had been built and new ways of

This old engraving of Norombega Hall dates from well before the building was burned in the fire of 1911. Many famous people, including presidents and actors, appeared on the building's stage in the nineteenth century. *Courtesy of Richard R. Shaw.*

marketing developed. By 1903, the Morey Furniture Co. planned to turn the old hall into a giant salesroom.

Designed by architect William Morse and built by his uncle Leonard Morse, the theater seated two thousand people on movable wooden benches on the floor, in galleries and even on the stage, but as many as three thousand had packed in for major events. "Wartime rallies, public fairs, receptions, balls, religious revivals and notable theatrical revivals made it the leading amusement center in the city," wrote the *Bangor Daily News* reporter.

Plenty of political rhetoric had echoed through the hall as well. People had come to hear Grant with such enthusiasm that the wooden platform at the front door had collapsed under the weight of the surging crowd. Benjamin Harrison and James Garfield had spoken there. There had been "a half dozen or so vice-presidents," including Bangor's favorite son, Hannibal Hamlin. Other great Maine political figures such as James G. Blaine, Thomas Brackett Reed and William Pitt Fessenden had also stood at the podium.

But it was the theatrical events that particularly struck the reporter as important. America's greatest nineteenth-century actor, Edwin Booth, brother of the country's most famous assassin, had performed *Hamlet* and other pieces over three nights. The beloved comedian Joseph Jefferson had played his most famous role, Rip Van Winkle.

This was the stage on which the city's Buskin Club had produced many plays beginning in the 1870s. The group had acquired a great deal of scenery, including a curtain portraying Yosemite Valley, painted by a Boston artist in one day. Buskin productions were so popular that theater enthusiasts would line up at night on the sidewalk in front of D. Bugbee & Co., the ticket vendor, to get the choicest seats when the store opened in the morning.

The residents of many cities yearn for a golden age that may exist mainly in their imaginations, and the reporter for the NEWS was no exception even at that relatively early date. After providing readers with a long list of famous actors and actresses who had graced the stage of Norombega Hall, he concluded, "We don't get such attractions now—dramatic art is not all that it used to be, perhaps."

By the end of its existence, "an unfortunate shop front addition" had impaired the building's lofty exterior, according to Deborah Thompson in her history of Bangor architecture. So perhaps it was actually a blessing of sorts when the wooden structure—devoid of purpose, its appearance marred—was destroyed in the great fire of 1911. In any event, the voices of Ulysses S. Grant and Edwin Booth still echo down the corridors of time for those park sitters among us with some imagination.

THE OPERA HOUSE AND THE AUDITORIUM

October 17, 2005

October a century ago was a memorable month in Bangor's theatrical and musical history. On October 9, Henrietta Crosman—"greatest of American actresses," asserted the *Bangor Daily News*—starred in *Mary, Mary, Quite Contrary* at the Opera House. The next night, James O'Neill reprised his signature role as the Count of Monte Cristo followed by Rose Coghlan in *The Duke of Killicrankie* the very next night.

All three actors were famous. Crosman's career spanned stage and screen through the 1930s. O'Neill was the father of Eugene, America's greatest playwright, and son immortalized Dad as the father character, James Tyrone, in *Long Days Journey into Night*.

These appearances by Broadway actors at the Opera House that October, however, were little compared to what was happening farther out on Main Street at the Bangor Auditorium, which a newspaper reporter once called

"Bangor's cherished temple of music." The ninth annual Maine Music Festival was featuring the state's own Emma Eames, world-famous opera diva, during its annual three-day extravaganza.

Back then, opera possessed a quasi-religious aura. Singers like Eames and Madame Lillian Nordica, another famous prima donna from Maine, were treated like goddesses. Queen City opera boosters had even built their own house of worship, the Bangor Auditorium, a mammoth, barn-like affair, 175 feet long and 82 feet wide, at the corner of Main and Buck Streets next to the Maplewood Park fairgrounds, just to house this annual fall event.

William R. Chapman, a New York choral director and Maine summer resident, was the musical spark behind the annual extravaganza. He had set out to create a "festival of choruses." Hundreds of singers representing dozens of communities from Houlton to Augusta gathered in Bangor, and later Portland, where the festival was also held, to provide a backup for the famous opera stars who appeared each fall. The incomparable Nordica had gotten things going in 1897, and now the beautiful Eames would shake the rafters along with several other well-known vocalists. "She is the one great star I have been trying for years to bring here," Chapman told the *Bangor Daily News* in January when his coup was announced more than eight months in advance of Eames's performance. "I hardly think the people of Maine realize what it means to the world of art that their state has given nearly as many singers of international fame and reputation as all the other states combined."

Born in China and raised in Bath, Eames had left Maine by the age of seventeen to train in Boston and then Europe. Like Nordica, who had performed at Bangor City Hall the previous winter, Eames told a reporter who visited her in her "prima donna suite" at the Bangor House that she was glad to be home. Unlike Nordica, she did not say she was looking forward one day to taking a vacation in the Maine woods. One got the feeling she had a preference for New York and Paris.

"Think of it—I have been so long away from Maine! All these years of study in Paris, and all those longer years of work in the great cities…I almost feel," said Madame with a move of her white hands, "as though when I walk along the street, I am surrounded by ghosts—the ghosts of other days."

Opposite, top: The original Bangor Opera House, which was located on Main Street, burned in 1914. *Courtesy of Richard R. Shaw.*

Opposite, bottom: The first Bangor Auditorium was located near the corner of Main and Buck Streets. *Courtesy of Richard R. Shaw.*

The reporter, who conducted the interview with fawning adoration, reminded the soprano that she had been "loyal to Maine," unlike the famous actress Maxine Elliott, who grew up in Rockland and allegedly never acknowledged her roots in the press.

The next afternoon, a reception was held at City Hall. There had been nothing like it in Bangor since the brilliant reception for Governor John F. Hill five years before, the newspaper reported. A score or more of "society young men" served as ushers, while the speakers included U.S. senator Eugene Hale.

The festival began in Bangor on October 5, on a Thursday evening, and consisted of five concerts, including two matinees, ending with a grand finale Saturday night featuring Eames when attendance was placed at 2,800. One could buy a ticket for all the concerts for five dollars or a ticket for just Eames's performance for anywhere from one dollar to three dollars, the equivalent of about sixty dollars today.

The Maine Music Festival ended in 1926, and the cavernous auditorium came down in 1967. But ghosts remain. Some months ago while browsing at an antique store in downtown Bangor, I found a pile of Maine Music Festival programs lying on the floor in the basement. Thinking I might have some use for one, I paid the cashier five dollars for the disintegrating 1905 edition, twenty times its price at the time it was issued, and the price of admission to all five concerts back then. Paging through, I found the mysterious spirit who purchased it had penciled parentheses around one piece—"Waltz" from *Romeo and Juliet* by Charles Gounod, Madame Emma Eames's first offering on that Saturday night long ago. This piece had special meaning for somebody. I like to think it helped prepare him or her for the long, cold winter ahead, and that this personage as well may have gone to see James O'Neill himself perform in something a little less lofty, something a bit warmer on the coming Tuesday night downtown at the Opera House.

GOING TO THE MOVIES: THE NICKEL AND THE GEM

February 4, 2008

Silent movies revolutionized entertainment in Bangor a century ago. The first full-time movie theater, the Nickel, opened in the new Graham Building on Central Street on August 12, 1907. Area people attended by

The Gaiety vaudeville theater was briefly located in old Norombega Hall on Central Street. In the next building was the Nickel, Bangor's first movie theater. Together they formed Bangor's Great White Way until the fire of 1911 destroyed both buildings. *Courtesy of Richard R. Shaw.*

the thousands—eighteen thousand during one early fall week alone, said the *Bangor Daily News* on September 23. Business was so good that the theater was enlarged. A big new lobby opened on January 4, 1908, so that waiting customers would no longer have to stand in the street.

Silent films were so popular that a second movie theater opened in February in the Blake Building at 164 Exchange Street. A contest was held to choose a name. The winner, Miss Eleanor Slattery of 120 Pearl Street, won a three-month free pass. Her choice, the Gem, became the name of Bangor's latest movie palace. It was located on the site of what would become the famed Bijou Theater just two years later as the city's array of entertainment resorts rapidly expanded.

The grand opening of the Gem was February 8. Both Bangor newspapers covered the event. Between noon and 11:00 p.m., three thousand people crowded into the theater to see repeat showings of *The Quack Doctor, Days of '61, Champion All the Same* and *The Sailor's Practical Joke*. Between shows, the Veilleux brothers, Philip and Dolor, sang the latest illustrated songs.

"With the most modern chairs, beautiful frescoing, rich velvet draperies and a delightful ladies room, it is certainly a 'Gem,'" reported the *Bangor Daily Commercial*. "The entrance is lighted by an arch supporting 257 incandescent lights, and the beautiful appearance in white and gold of the front of the theater will be noticeable. Swinging doors at each side of the box office admit the public to the auditorium. Every seat has a complete view of the picture." (In less than a week, the management announced it was going to raise the stage two feet so everybody could see.)

The little orchestra pit had space for piano player Ralph Fortier and a drummer. Special attention was paid to fire safety. "The room where the machines [projectors] are arranged is lined with sheet steel with an asbestos backing," added the paper. The movies would change every other day, the illustrated songs twice a week.

Meanwhile, a block or two away, throngs continued to pack the Nickel, which had more than double the seating capacity of the Gem. On the same day the Gem opened, the *Bangor Daily News* reported that the Nickel had "big crowds all day long, plenty of laughter and applause…that's the story in a nutshell." Enthusiasm for the movies seemed to know no boundaries.

Another new development reflecting the entertainment revolution was the opening of the Queen City's first penny arcade on September 30, 1907, on Central Street. "One side of the long room is occupied by phonograph or song machines, while picture machines fill the other. In all there are 60 of these machines." An electric automatic rifle and target was featured along with a Fairbanks Standard Scale, which gave weight and height along with a variety of strength tests. A huge teddy bear, "advertising that very popular song 'Won't You Be My Teddy Bear?'" was stationed by a big show window on the street, reported the *Bangor Daily News* on opening day.

But the most exciting news—or rumor—was that Bangor was about to get its first vaudeville theater, operated by the Keith theater syndicate. On December 2, 1907, the *Bangor Daily News* explained the situation: "The magnificent new Keith theater in Portland is nearing completion, and another Keith theater is soon to be opened in St. John, the same artists appearing at each." Bangor would be the city in the middle to break up the journey for the same quality performers as the bigger cities.

The Keiths were proposing that local capitalists build a theater and lease it to them. One of those wealthy men, John R. Graham, who owned the building in which the Nickel was located, denied a rumor he was buying land on which to build the new theater, reported the *Bangor Daily News* on December 28. The Keiths already had a relationship with Graham. The president of the Bangor Nickel Corporation was A. Paul Keith, a top company official.

Another site discussed was the old Norombega Hall, which sat in the Kenduskeag Stream between Central and Franklin Streets. The stage had been removed several years ago, and renovations would be expensive. A. Paul Keith visited Bangor to inspect the old theater, where such famous actors as Joseph Jefferson and Edwin Booth had performed in a previous era, the *Bangor Daily News* reported February 6, 1908. Bangor people were amusement hungry. "In fact, Bangor has long been recognized as the best show town in all New England," the reporter asserted hopefully.

The folks who ran the Bangor Opera House, the city's bastion of live dramatic performances, must have watched these developments with trepidation. Advertisements now called the theater "The New Bangor Opera House" since major renovations were completed some months before. How the theater would be affected by the growing number of low-priced movie houses and a new vaudeville theater was unknown.

Of course, it would adapt to prevailing tastes. The week the Gem opened, the Opera House was featuring a movie at "a special low price" of only ten cents. The next week, a vaudeville company was booked.

THE QUEEN CITY'S FIRST VAUDEVILLE HOUSE

October 27, 2008

Bangor's first vaudeville theater opened with a glittering social affair on Monday evening, October 26, 1908, a century ago this week. Union Hall, located on Union Street facing the Bangor House, had been transformed into the Union Theater, "a tasteful little vaudeville house," according to the *Bangor Daily News.*

Vaudeville was a relatively new phenomenon that lasted from the 1890s to the 1930s. For a city its size, Bangor was late in getting its own vaudeville theater, so imagine the excitement that first night. Tickets were by invitation only. A "ladies orchestra" directed by Miss Margaret Cassidy, pianist, warmed up the audience, while "charming young women, all gowned in white" ushered. This all-female effect was considered quite innovative.

Harry I. Bolton, president of the Bangor Bowling and Amusement Company, which owned the theater building, was invited up to the stage to receive "a handsome bouquet from the jewelers of Bangor." After the orchestra played an overture, and a projectionist in a booth lined with asbestos showed a brief moving picture about South Africa, the real fun began. "A Dutch comedian in dialogue," a wooden shoe dancer and a

This building, a former roller-skating rink on Union Street, successively became the Union, Acker's Family, the Nickel and the Olympia Theaters before a fire destroyed it. *Courtesy of Richard R. Shaw.*

singing and dancing soubrette (a saucy, coquettish maidservant in comic operas, according to my dictionary) opened the show.

After these preliminaries, Ferrari, the handcuff king, dazzled the audience with his ability to get out of all sorts of locked situations. Wesley Norris and Stella Wiley, colored comedians, singers and dancers, got an enthusiastic ovation. Then came the highlight of the show, the Rosaires, wirewalkers. Mr. Rosaire was billed as the only man in the country who could do a swinging handstand on a slack wire.

Union Hall had been dedicated twenty-two years before as a roller-skating rink. After that craze died away, it became a furniture store, then "the home of polo" and finally a bowling and billiard hall, according to the *Bangor Daily News* on October 27. Now vaudeville would have its day.

Vaudeville had preceded movies in most cities, but now movies were putting some of the vaudeville theaters out of business. Not in Bangor. Two movie theaters had recently opened, the Nickel in August 1907 and the Gem in February 1908. "That there is a field for a vaudeville house here nobody will dispute," Harry M. Gardner, manager of the new theater, explained to the *Bangor Daily News* on September 11 before the theater opened. "You will have to travel the length and breadth of the United States to find another city with an immediate drawing population of 45,000 to 50,000 people which has nothing between the 'legitimate' [stage plays such as those performed at the Bangor Opera House] on the one hand and moving pictures on the other. This is an abnormal theatrical condition."

Bangor would be part of a vaudeville circuit that included Lowell, Lynn and Salem, Massachusetts, as well as Portland, Gardiner, Augusta, Waterville and Fairfield, Maine, St. John N.B. and perhaps some other cities. Advertisements promised "high-class" vaudeville, "a strong bill and a clean one," a reference to the vulgar humor associated with many vaudeville acts. Tickets were ten, twenty and thirty cents, and the four shows, lasting for two and a half hours each, stretched from noon to 10:30 p.m., according to plans announced in the newspapers.

The transformation of Union Hall was a marvel to behold. The front of the building, finished in green and gold, was to have the distinction of being "the first theater in New England to be fitted on the mission style of architecture." That style, as interpreted by local architect W.E. Mansur, featured towers on each end of the front of the building. His creation became one of Bangor's most venerable entertainment institutions for fifty years.

Inside was a large lobby with the ticket office and stairs leading up to the main auditorium and horseshoe balcony. The theater would seat eight hundred or one thousand people, according to various newspaper accounts. Eight fire escapes secured by "glass locks" allowed easy exit in case of fire, always a major concern back when theater fires were widely reported in the newspapers.

A maze of green lattice work on the walls and ceiling cut by a series of broad, white arches and decorated with masses of palms, shrubs and flowers was intended to give the audience the impression they were watching the stage from inside a huge arbor. "Green, white and gold will be the predominant tints," declared the *Bangor Daily News* in describing this contrivance on October 5.

This was truly Bangor's golden age of entertainment. The Union Theater was Bangor's fourth theater, and three more were in various stages of creation, according to the newspapers. These included the enlargement and redesign of the Gem, the rehabilitation of the old Norombega Theater, which had been dormant for a number of years, and the construction of a new theater at York and Exchange Streets.

How was all this going to affect the Bangor Opera House, still the city's premier vendor of high-brow theatrical drama (although it occasionally let movies and vaudeville acts sneak onto its stage)? Things were better than ever, according to the end-of-the-year wrap up in the *Bangor Daily News* on January 1, 1909: "The past year has brought a radical change in the local theatrical situation, and it is a change which benefits the play-going public." The low-quality repertory shows, which often performed a different play every night for a week, were being edged out by the movie and vaudeville "craze." The flip side of the coin, however, was that more "good shows," featuring famous actors and Broadway and near-Broadway plays with the original casts, were being booked at the Opera House in an effort to cater to more sophisticated theater lovers.

As for the Union Theater, it lasted barely a year. Acker's Family Theater, part of a Canadian company, had replaced it by 1909. Then the Nickel took over the building after its home on Central Street was destroyed in the fire of 1911. Finally, around 1920, the Olympia, which is still remembered by many Bangoreans today, operated there until the late 1950s. The building was gutted in a fire on November 19, 1963.

THE BIJOU: BANGOR'S FINEST THEATER

April 16, 2012

Bangor's most elegant theater—more glamorous today to many because it was torn down shortsightedly during Urban Renewal—had its grand opening a century ago this week. The *Titanic* had sunk a few days before, but doubtlessly for some who attended, the hoopla surrounding the Bijou's second coming would dominate their memories of that week in history for years to come.

This wasn't the first Bijou. A smaller vaudeville house by the same name had opened in the same location at 164 Exchange Street two years before (replacing an earlier theater, the Gem). The second Bijou was so much more grandiose that April 18, 1912, came to be regarded as its official birth by most sources.

The re-opening of the Bijou and the opening of a second new theater, the Palace, which began showing movies nearby at 95 Exchange Street in early February, were just the latest signs that Bangor's economy was still hot after the big fire that destroyed fifty-five downtown acres the previous April. The fire destroyed two Central Street theaters, the old Norombega Hall (which contained the Gaiety vaudeville house) and the Nickel, the city's first movie theater.

But nothing could keep theaters down in that era. The Nickel soon moved to a theater building on Union Street, while the expanded Bijou absorbed

Right: The Bijou Theater a decade or so after it was built. *Courtesy of Richard R. Shaw.*

Below: The Bijou's interior. *Courtesy of Richard R. Shaw.*

the functions of the Gaiety. All three theaters were operated by the powerful Keith theater chain, which, it was believed, would reward Bangor for its enthusiastic backing of popular entertainment by sending a higher class of vaudeville to the Queen City on a par with Portland and Boston. That was the promise. "Our vaudeville will be much better than we had at the old Bijou. We shall have all of the important acts this spring which play the Keith theater in Portland," theater manager Steve Bogrett told a reporter for the *Bangor Daily News* on March 28 as the new Bijou neared completion.

There was plenty of cash around to finance new theaters. There was room for all classes of entrepreneurs. The Palace was built by Pope D. McKinnon, proprietor of the Globe Hotel, which was located in a rundown neighborhood on French Street.

"The Pope" was an aficionado of horse racing and liquor dealing, having had more than one run-in with the police. He hoped to use a hall upstairs for boxing exhibitions and dancing. He considered himself a connoisseur of movie-house singers. "It's a hobby of mine," he told the *Bangor Daily News* on September 14, 1911.

The Bijou was owned by Edward H. Blake, a scion of great wealth as well as a former Bangor mayor. A lawyer and a composer of music and poetry, Blake was president of the Merchants National Bank, a large stockholder at the *Bangor Daily News*, which was located next to the theater, and a major downtown property owner. A prominent yachtsman, he held memberships in several yacht clubs as well as Bangor's famed Tarratine Club. Blake's theater was leased by the Keiths. The theater building was extended back to the Kenduskeag Stream and widened to take over space previously occupied by a storehouse belonging to a shoe company. It was decorated to a level of ornateness never before seen in Bangor. Opening night was a grand

Edward H. Blake. *Courtesy of the Bangor Museum and History Center.*

affair, so grand that the reporter assigned by the *Bangor Daily News* had to strain to find enough superlatives:

> *Long lines of automobiles were drawn up in Exchange Street, and for an hour, their faultlessly attired occupants streamed beneath the blazing circles and pyramids of lights which made the street bright as day. It was a remarkable scene in the big auditorium—big, yet with a skillfully conveyed sense of coziness and intimacy—a splendid audience...set amid surroundings of old rose and ivory, of beautiful paintings and massive plastic relief.*

Exclamations of surprise could be heard inside the theater at the "lavish luxury displayed on every side," the reporter continued.

> *The little cupids and seashells in plastic relief adorning the front of the balcony; the life-sized feminine figures surmounting the boxes; the immense painting—glowing, graceful groups in the semi-nude against an azure background—which glorifies the great sweep of the outer proscenium arch; the massive centerpiece* ["a large ornamental light hanging from the ceiling drop and about it...four globes throwing light upon the ceiling"], *which one could admire for hours and not waste his time; the deep rose and old ivory wonderfully blending in the color scheme; the whole reflected in the golden gleam of myriads of concealed lights.... [Eight] clean-looking young ushers, in the conventional Keith uniform of very deep blue, with black braid and gilt-lettered caps, were drawn up at the head of each long aisle.*

The show, five acts accompanied by an orchestra directed by Emile Beauparlant, was thought to be a notch above the typical vaudeville Bangoreans had come to expect. Every act came direct from a major Keith theater in either Boston, Lowell, Lynn or Portland, said the papers. But the content of these performances today sounds remarkably similar to what had been playing in Bangor vaudeville houses since the first one opened in 1908.

A "playlet" called *The Bandit*, starring E. Frederick Hawley, a well-known vaudeville star, topped the list. The Venetian Four, violinists and a harpist, performed "A Night in Venice," set against various romantic backdrops. Other acts included Barnes & Robinson in "a mélange of music and song;" Edward Estus, the "acme of athletic artistry"—a "sensational equilibrist;" and Speigel & Dunn, blackface comedians, a staple of vaudeville in those days. The performances were interspersed with movie shorts.

Within a few months, Bangoreans would be able to see both Mae West and Will Rogers on the Bijou's stage.

The theaters of the day were democratic institutions. Prices at the new Bijou ranged from ten cents to twenty-five cents depending on whether one sat in the balcony or in a box over the stage. Almost anyone could afford to see one of the three daily performances.

The proliferation of electric bulbs played a major role as well in making the Bijou the most glamorous place in town.

"THOUSANDS OF LIGHTS ADORN NEW THEATER," proclaimed a headline in the *Bangor Daily News* on April 1. A twenty-two-foot-high sign spelling out the theater's name in light bulbs and surmounted by a blazing star could be seen up and down Exchange Street. "Serpentine effects"—"flashes of yellow fire"—ran up and down the sign, the reporter wrote, struggling for words. On top of the building and out back over the Kenduskeag Stream, more lighted signs and effects made it difficult to be anywhere downtown without experiencing Bangor's Great White Way.

"Bangor now has what it has long desired, a first-class, up-to-date vaudeville house, where the best features of the vaudeville world will be presented. The opening of the new house marks the beginning of a new theatrical era in Bangor," concluded the *Bangor Daily Commercial* the day after the opening. Had the newspaper reporter been able to read the future, however, he might have changed the word "beginning" to "pinnacle." Knowing what we know about the course of popular entertainment, it would have been easy to count the years until the Queen City found itself unable to maintain its multitude of old-fashioned theaters and their glorious mix of live plays, movies, vaudeville and opera.

Chapter 3
DISASTERS, TRAGEDIES AND MAYHEM

SIX BANGOR BOYS DIED IN SAILING ACCIDENT

July 9, 2007

SIX BANGOR BOYS DROWNED IN BAY: Sloop Yacht *Ruth E.*
Cumnock Capsized in Squall on Tuesday and All But One of Party of Seven Lost; THRILLING TALE OF SOLE SURVIVOR.

This multi-tiered headline in the *Bangor Daily News* announced one of the great tragedies in Bangor history. Drownings were a common occurrence, but this event hit the Queen City hard.

A century ago today, seven vacationing young men, all graduates or students of Bangor High School, were sailing in a thirty-eight-foot sloop from Stockton Springs to Isleboro when they were suddenly tossed into the choppy waters of Penobscot Bay "off Castine back cove about half a mile above Dice's Head." Only Loren D. Hall returned to tell the story. This column is taken from several newspaper pieces, but primarily from the account provided by Hall to the *Bangor Daily Commercial* on July 11, 1907, two days after the accident.

Plans for the outing were made the night before, when Hall and several others vacationing at the Hersey Retreat, a large church-sponsored cottage on Sandy Point, were down at the steamboat wharf as their friends Harry Dugan, a Bowdoin College sophomore, and Charlie Wood showed up on

The original Hersey Retreat in Stockton Springs was owned by the First Universalist Church in Bangor. *Courtesy of Richard R. Shaw.*

the steamer *Tremont* from Bangor. Dugan and Wood were on their way to Castine to meet Billy Veague, who was the youthful master of the *Ruth E. Cumnock.*

Harry and Charlie planned to return with Veague and his yacht the next day for a sail in the bay before attending a dance that night at the Retreat. Veague, who was living across the bay in South Brooksville, was a recent graduate of Pratt Institute. His father was master of a large steam yacht. Dugan was the only son of a dealer in harnesses and trunks. Hall's father was a grocery store owner.

The next day, Harry and Billy appeared on the sailboat about noon at Sandy Point. Charlie Wood stayed in Castine trying to ready his own launch for travel. He survived because of this delay.

Besides Hall, Dugan and Veague, the sailing party included Roy Palmer, son of the storekeeper at the Eastern Maine Insane Hospital; Frederick Ringwall, son of a noted Bangor musician who was in Sweden with his wife visiting his family; Amos Robinson, son of the superintendent of motive power for the Maine Central Railroad; and Ray Smith, son of a traveling salesman. Ringwall was a student at the University of Maine, where he was an accomplished musician.

At the outset, there wasn't much wind, but it was a great day for a sail, recalled Hall. Billy Veague was giving Harry Dugan sailing lessons. After running down to Fort Point, they headed out into the bay seeking more wind. The plan was to go to Hewes Point on Isleboro and return to Sandy Point by 5:30 p.m.

Out in the bay, the wind freshened. "The water was flying some, and we were having a great time," Hall told the *Commercial* reporter. "The wind was blowing from the northwest. It was light and blowing steady. We had the main sail, stay sail and jib set. The yacht carried a topsail, too, but we didn't have that set."

Part way down the bay, black clouds began to roll up. The boys thought they might have a thundershower. "We were wet some then, so we didn't care if it did rain," said Hall. Roy Palmer and Hall were forward, and the rest of the fellows were in the cockpit. Harry was at the wheel, and Billy was standing not three feet from him. (Earlier press reports also based on reports of conversations with Hall had stated Billy had left the wheel area momentarily at the time of the accident.) "The squall struck us without any warning at all. The boat heeled over and at the very first dip—I guess she took in five or six hogsheads of water," said Hall. There wasn't enough time to release the sails. In moments, the sloop was flat over on her side, the sails in the water. Then she sank quickly.

The end came within minutes for most of the boys. Freddy Ringwall and Harry Dugan, who was immediately thrown from the yacht, couldn't swim. Roy Palmer could swim only a little, but he gamely struck off for shore. Ray Smith was badly injured. Veague and Hall, who were both strong swimmers, tried to hold him up but abandoned the futile effort. Hall struck off for shore using an oar to stay afloat, but it slowed him down so he left it behind. He passed Amos Robinson, who was clutching a seat from the yacht's tender. After Hall passed him, Amos called out for help, saying he had a cramp. Hall said he was unable to return to him in the heavy seas, which he estimated to be five or six feet high.

Meanwhile, the tugboat *Bismarck* was returning to Bangor from a towing job. Hall had been in the water for about forty-five minutes and was still far from shore. He had a cramp in his right leg, and he was exhausted. At the sight of the tug, he began to shout. Two crew members heard him, and a rescue was underway.

When the *Bismarck* returned Hall to the Hersey Retreat, all the young people were in the hall preparing for the dance. Amos Robinson's sister Martha recalled:

> *When he appeared in the room, we all asked, "Where are all the boys?" "They're all drowned but me," said Loren, and he walked through the room and upstairs. We laughed and didn't think anything of it for a minute. But soon we noticed that Loren wasn't around. Someone ran upstairs and found him up there crying. He came down and proceeded to tell about the accident. No one went to bed that night at the retreat. We simply sat around and talked and waited for morning to come. We couldn't believe that all the boys had been drowned. We all went down to meet the Tremont Wednesday morning when she came in, hoping, but way down in our hearts not believing, that some of the boys would be onboard.*

The deaths of six middle-class youths with promising futures unnerved the people of Bangor. A proclamation of mourning was issued by city dignitaries. Some of the richest men in Bangor donated money to finance a search for bodies. The *Ruth E. Cumnock* was found on July 30 off Perkins Point in Castine. Bodies were discovered in the days ahead, and funerals were held.

Four of the boys had attended the Universalist Church, which owned the Hersey Retreat. As the rain fell in torrents outside the church on the day of one of the funerals, the minister spoke of "the mystery of death, of the constant, persistent and unanswerable questions that have existed from creation." These same thoughts doubtlessly were on the minds of the hundreds of mourners as well.

MURDER AT AUNT HAT'S?

February 18, 2008

Harriet Foyer operated the most notorious bordello in the Bangor area a century ago, just over the city line in Veazie on a spot overlooking the Penobscot River. Like Fan Jones, her famous predecessor, much romantic folderol has been spun about Aunt Hat, as she was known far and wide. But the trial of two of her hired thugs for manslaughter in February 1908 reveals that old Hat was less endearing than her popular image.

"The mystery of a dark and stormy night at a lonely road house—the mystery of how Fred Bunker came to his death—was investigated in the supreme court on Thursday afternoon, and a great throng was present to follow the details," the *Bangor Daily News* reported on February 14, the morning after the opening of the trial of Hat's bouncer, Frank "Frenchy" Parrent, and another employee, Wesley Collins, in Bangor.

Fred B. Bunker of North Sullivan had come to Bangor on Labor Day to celebrate with two friends. Each carried a quart of whiskey that they consumed as the day went by. All three men were granite cutters. Possibly they had marched in the Labor Day parade that morning in Bangor. In the afternoon, they decided to take the trolley up State Street to Aunt Hat's isolated place for supper and a night of carousing.

When they got off the trolley near Mount Hope Cemetery, they encountered Frenchy Parrent, a convicted criminal also known as Kid Doyle to local boxing fans. Parrent offered to guide them to the famed roadhouse on the Shore Road overlooking the river. After being greeted by the venerable Aunt Hat, the group spent a few minutes in the parlor, where one of them played a few tunes on the piano before they retired to the dining room.

That's when the trouble started. For reasons never explained, Bunker, who was very drunk, took a swing at his companion, Wallace Springer, giving him a bloody nose. Springer jumped from the table and ran out the door. Bunker either chased after him or was physically ejected from the house by Parrent and Collins. Aunt Hat made it clear to her boys she wanted him out because he was drunk and troublesome. He had also failed to pay for his drinks even though he was supposed to be carrying a great wad of cash.

Parrent and Collins were observed by several witnesses, some as far away as the other side of the river in North Brewer, chasing and throwing rocks at Bunker until the granite cutter fell into the bushes some distance from the house. A great deal of inconclusive court testimony failed to determine how many rocks actually hit Bunker or what might have happened after he disappeared from sight.

Aunt Hat forbade Bunker's friends from bringing him back to the house. "To hell with him," she supposedly replied to Collins when he suggested they should go check up on him because he might fall in the river.

Later that night, near the Red Bridge district of Bangor about a mile south of Aunt Hat's, Bunker's mutilated body was found on the Bangor Railway & Electric Company tracks after having been hit by a northbound trolley. Had he been murdered or beaten unconscious and dumped on the tracks, or had he crawled there on his own?

The condition of Bunker's body was cited as evidence by County Attorney Hervey Patten that he had been beaten to death before his body was left on the tracks. "Old railroad men who have witnessed many accidents will tell you that when a man is killed—even though he should be cut in two—the flesh will quiver for some time. There will be some movement—some sign of vitality," Patten told the jury. "But in this case, the body was absolutely motionless. Furthermore, the blood upon the face was dried, as though it had been there for hours."

The prosecutor suddenly withdrew the manslaughter charge the next day, however. No one had actually seen Parrent and Collins hitting Bunker. No one had seen them drag his body to the spot on the tracks where he was found.

The most damaging witness for the defense was William Landry of Veazie, a passenger on the trolley that ran over Bunker. He testified he heard Bunker gasp as he lay dying on the tracks, and that someone else had said something about the man taking his last breath.

Parrent and Collins were convicted of assault and battery. They were each sentenced to a year in the county jail, "allowances being made for their youth," reported the *Bangor Daily News* on February 25.

On the opening morning of the trial, Aunt Hat made what apparently was her only appearance at the proceedings. She was arraigned on a charge of maintaining "a common nuisance." We have this description of her from a *Bangor Daily News* reporter: "With hair almost snow white and gowned in deep black, she hobbled on crutches to the prisoner's box, where in response to the reading of the indictment, she feebly pleaded 'not guilty.' She was then assisted to a seat before the judge's stand, and while her bondsmen were being examined, her sobs shook the courtroom. The bail was satisfactory, and Mrs. Foyer left the court with an attendant supporting her on either side." The charges were later dropped, according to court records.

Aunt Hat had faced similar charges before. Her histrionics, however, may not have been completely insincere. In her late sixties, she was nearing the end of her career. The legal establishment was trying to put her out of business once and for all. She may still have been recovering emotionally from the death of her nine-year-old granddaughter, Hazel, who had been struck by a Maine Central Railroad train last June opposite the upper entrance to Mount Hope Cemetery.

The court testimony of Ross J. Murphy, another of Hat's employees, provides additional insights into Aunt Hat's nature. Murphy, who had been brought in on a separate, unrelated assault charge, worked as a "spieler" and a ticket taker for Hat's tent shows at fairs where her girls danced. The morning after Labor Day, Hat sent Murphy to the site of Bunker's assault, where he searched unsuccessfully for the money the granite cutter was alleged to have been carrying. Parrent and Collins, who told Murphy they had given Bunker "an awful beating," claimed they did not have the cash.

Bunker's fancy derby hat, with the initials F.B.B. on the hatband, had been retrieved from the scene earlier, and Aunt Hat gave it to Murphy as a little bonus, telling him not to reveal where he got it. Murphy wore the hat at the fairs where he worked that fall before trading it for a cap at Chesuncook Lake when he went to work in the woods as a logger. Later, it was seized as evidence by authorities.

One can conclude from this and other testimony that Aunt Hat probably ordered the attack on Bunker to obtain his money, which would have paid for far more than the cost of his drinks. While Hat may not have ordered

Bunker's murder, her callousness in neglecting the drunken granite cutter after he had received "an awful beating" at the hands of her thugs contributed to the events leading up to his death. The trial publicity no doubt did great damage to Aunt Hat's business in its waning days.

BANGOR'S FIRST AUTO FATALITY

June 2, 2008

The first fatal automobile accident in the Bangor area occurred a century ago this week on State Street. It was a warm spring evening after 8:00 p.m. on June 4, 1908. Harold Colby, a chauffeur, had dropped off his employer, Thomas R. Savage, at his home at 191 Broadway after a drive out to Pushaw Pond. Colby, nineteen, had been in Savage's employ for about three weeks.

The wealthy wholesale grocer had told his young driver many times to always take his red, thirty-five-horsepower, five-passenger Pope Hartford machine back to A.B. Purington's garage on Exchange Street when it was not being used by the Savage family. Savage said he also had told Colby never to go more than ten or twelve miles per hour, in keeping with the speed limits of the day.

Colby was an experienced chauffeur, having driven for four years, but he had other things on his mind that night. After dropping off Savage, he drove back down Broadway to State. Instead of turning right toward downtown and the garage, he turned left toward Fruit Street, where Alice Curran lived. He and Miss Curran talked on her front steps for awhile, and then, at about 8:20 p.m., went for a short ride up to Mount Hope Avenue, where he turned the auto around and brought the young woman home. She noticed that the vehicle's acetylene headlamps were not working, unlike on other evening jaunts they had made. But it was not quite dark yet.

At about 8:30 p.m. (or a bit later or earlier, depending on whose story you believed), Colby headed back to State Street, where he turned right toward downtown. At about the same time, ten-year-old Freddie O'Connor, his older brother Charlie and a friend, Lawrence Moore, were walking up State Street on the sidewalk. The Moore boy was running an errand to the Essex Pharmacy on State Street, and the O'Connors accompanied him. Freddie and Charlie lived on Otis Street, where their father ran a junk business.

When the boys were across the street from St. Xavier's Convent (where the former St. John's School building is located today), Freddie darted across the street. Colby was moving along at a good clip of about twenty miles per hour or more with no lights, according to several witnesses. This part of the street was dark because of the massive elm trees towering above it and because the nearest street lamps were some distance away. The speed limit was eight miles per hour. Auto headlamps were supposed to be lit one hour after sunset, which would have been by 8:39 p.m. that night, according to later testimony.

When Freddie O'Connor ran in front of him, Colby said he slammed on the vehicle's two sets of brakes, pushed in the clutch and skidded nearly to a stop, narrowly missing the boy. The youngster bounded part way up the steep embankment leading to the sidewalk in front of the convent, but then, inexplicably, he jumped back into the street right in front of the auto just as Colby accelerated.

People walking near the accident said they heard what sounded like a tire burst. The glass in the headlamp smashed. Colby said he knew he had hit a person or a dog, but he kept on driving, planning to take the auto to the garage and then return to the scene of the accident. The story was further

Bangor's first automobile fatality occurred in front of the Convent of Mercy on State Street. *Courtesy of Richard R. Shaw.*

complicated by another auto going in the opposite direction. Did its lights blind or confuse the victim or the driver momentarily?

A passerby carried Freddie to the nearby home of Dr. Harold Crane. Awhile later, the boy was taken to Eastern Maine General Hospital in the arms of an officer in the city's horse-drawn police ambulance. He died early the next morning.

Police immediately went in search of the auto and driver. They soon found the vehicle at Purington's, recognizing it by the broken lamp. The driver was gone, however. Colby had walked back to State Street, encountered Miss Curran and asked her to go inquire about the accident. When he learned that a boy had been badly injured, he said he determined to turn himself in to police.

At 10:00 p.m., accompanied by Savage and his parents, Colby arrived at the police station. After spending a night in jail, he was arraigned in municipal court on a charge of involuntary manslaughter the next day. He pleaded not guilty and secured bail of $2,000. Later, he visited the O'Connor family with his parents.

Reaction was swift in the city's two daily newspapers. The *Bangor Daily Commercial*, which had been complaining for months that auto regulations were inadequate, charged in an editorial on June 8 that even the current laws weren't being enforced. The writer implied Colby and his employer had been guilty of speeding on previous occasions. When a policeman was asked why he hadn't enforced the speeding law, he said "he did not like to complain against the owner of the auto, who is a prominent citizen."

Colby was tried seven months later before a packed courtroom. Before taking the stand to testify, he wept silently, and so did many others in the courtroom. "'Brace up,' said his lawyer, P.H. Gillin. 'Put on a brave front. Be a man.' At this the prisoner resolutely wiped his eyes, blew his nose and walked to the stand," reported the *Bangor Daily News*. His lawyer had the last words:

> *The sole cause of the boy's injury could not have been laid to the fault of Colby, even if there had been fault. Here was a boy of 10 or 12 who deliberately ran out into the public street, through which car after car, and vehicle after vehicle, were passing. And he ran, all young and white and spotless as he was, straight into the arms of the Almighty, leaving this other boy with a burning spot upon his mind and soul—forever. It was the act of the dead boy, and not of the poor unfortunate living boy, which has brought us here today.*

When the jury found Colby not guilty, "a great wave of applause swept over the courtroom, and no one tried to stop it," reported the *Bangor Daily News* on February 12, 1909. Bangor had never experienced such an event before, but there would be plenty more in the future as the automobile became a popular means of transportation among all classes of people.

COP KILLER

November 24, 2008

DIED AT THOMASTON—Career of W.H. Albert Ends at State Prison

Officer Patrick Henry Jordan, the victim.

This headline in the *Bangor Daily Commercial* on November 28, 1908, a century ago this week, marked the conclusion of one of the most heinous criminal careers in Bangor history. William H. Albert had murdered Patrolman Patrick Henry Jordan, a family man with six children, just five years ago. Jordan, thirty-five at the time of his death, had been on the beat for less than a week when Albert shot him in the face during a chase. Now the murderer, who had appeared healthy and strong at the time of the crime, was dead as well.

William and Hannah Albert were divorced. His ex-wife was terrified of him. The burly blacksmith, always identified as a Negro or colored in newspaper stories, had recently served ninety days in jail for assaulting an elderly man. He was also "afflicted with the detective mania," said the *Bangor Daily News*. He had obtained a badge and credentials from an organization called the American Detective Agency. He claimed to have had in his possession five revolvers, according to testimony at the coroner's inquest on Jordan's death.

On Saturday, March 7, 1903, after a night of drinking, Albert decided to pay Hannah a visit. She lived at 1 St. Michael's Court (Second Street Avenue), a narrow lane off Second Street near Union. When she heard her husband outside her house late that night as she lay in bed, she blew out the lamp hoping he would go away. When he started pounding on the door, she jumped from a second-story window in her nightgown. She ran to a home on Second Street, begging the resident to call the police on his telephone. It was about 11:00 p.m. The wheels of justice started to turn.

Patrolman Jordan walked briskly to the scene from Franklin

William Albert, the murderer.

Street, where he was on duty. Patrolman Thomas O'Donohue came up in the paddy wagon. While Jordan guarded the front door on St. Michael's Court, O'Donohue searched the house. When he entered Hannah Albert's bedroom, her ex-husband jumped out the same window from which she had escaped into the vacant lot below.

A maze of alleys and streets converged in the area. Neither police officer had any idea which way Albert might have gone—whether to Sanford, Union, Second or Cedar Streets. After a few minutes of fruitless searching, O'Donohue returned to the stable with the wagon. He assumed Jordan might have caught the culprit and gone back to the police station.

The exact route of Jordan's determined chase after Albert remains unknown. One witness encountered Jordan coming from Sanford Street onto Cedar Street in pursuit of someone who had just run through his yard between 11:00 and 11:30 p.m. After that sighting, the *Bangor Daily News* surmised, "It is probable the two men went through Plum Street [off Cedar] to Parker and up Parker to the wool factory at the end of Fourth Street, for at this point, a man and woman were standing who saw the negro pass them. Then he went into Hellier's Brickyard [at Fourth and Parker]. The patrolman was hot on the trail though, and a young man who was at the head of Carroll Street saw the negro dart past him running for dear life from the brickyard with Jordan a few feet behind him."

Meanwhile, Raynsford Talbot was helping his father, Charles, move scenery from the Bangor Opera House. He started for their home on Carroll Street, leaving his father at his stable on Fourth. When he turned onto Carroll Street, he was startled to see what appeared to be a body lying across the sidewalk near the intersection with Third. He went back to get his father, who notified police.

"It's another man. It isn't Henry," said one of the first policemen on the scene. But Patrolman O'Donohue went closer and lifted up one of the arms. "My God," he cried. "There's the star. It's the boy."

A shot had been heard by neighbors, but no one had seen anything. Within forty minutes of the time Raynsford Talbot found Jordan's body, Police Chief John Bowen and a squad of eight policemen were getting ready to close in on the fugitive.

At about 11:30 p.m., Albert had begun pounding and kicking on the door and window of the home of Mr. and Mrs. Jesse Huddlan at 106 Walter Street, not far from the scene of the crime. He was flourishing a gun and seemed paralyzed with fear one moment and boastful the next. "I've shot a policeman," he said. "They are after me, and I want you to hide me. I killed him."

The Huddlans hadn't seen Albert for two years. They told him to lie on the floor in the hopes that he would go to sleep. He pleaded with them not to leave him alone. Mrs. Huddlan was too frightened to sleep. Taking her baby, she slipped out a window and went to Fire Station 2, where firemen called the police.

As the men were getting ready to surround the Huddlan house, Chief Bowen made a short speech as reported in the *Bangor Daily News*: "Now boys, there is a man in there who has probably done murder once tonight, and I don't want you to take any chances. Draw your guns, and if he attempts to shoot, trim him."

The house was in darkness. Thanks to Mrs. Huddlan, the police knew Albert was probably on the floor near the front door. Patrolman Harry

Baker crawled up the front steps and pushed open the door without a sound. Patrolmen Fred Perkins and John Finnigan were close behind. Perkins showed a light. There was Albert a few feet away, lying on his side motionlessly, a gun in his right hand.

Baker grabbed his arm, wrestling the weapon from him, while Perkins pinned down his head, whisking out his handcuffs. Together the two men applied the manacles.

A crowd waited at the station when the police arrived with Albert at 12:50 a.m. He was rushed into the cell room, where Captain John Mackie supervised a search. "Mackie," the murderer cried. "Mackie, you know me—say, in God's name, what is this? For God's sakes boys, what am I up for?"

These were violent times for Bangor cops. Patrolman Thomas Davis and his family were lucky to escape death a few weeks later when someone tried to blow up their house on Johnson Street while they were sleeping. Other police officers were assaulted by thugs as they tried to quell drunken mobs in this era before police cars and two-way radios. But the death of Officer Jordan remained the worst assault on the Bangor Police Department for years to come.

"GAMBLE WITH DEATH" CAUSED TRAIN WRECK

July 25, 2011

Two passenger trains steamed toward each other during a violent storm along a remote stretch of track north of Millinocket on the evening of July 28, 1911, a century ago this week. In the head-on crash that followed between the excursion train heading to Caribou from Searsport and the regular passenger train from Van Buren to Bangor, nine people died and two dozen more were injured. It was the worst wreck in the history of the Bangor and Aroostook Railroad, and one of the worst in Maine history.

The twenty-one-member Presque Isle Community Band was the sponsor of the annual excursion train to Penobscot Park, the B&A's amusement center at the end of its seaport route in Searsport. Just before the crash, most of the band members were sitting in a car at the head of the train just behind the locomotive's coal tender. Band members were preparing to serenade a member of a local baseball team who had been injured that day during a game at the park. Bandleader Charles Palmer lifted his baton, and the musicians raised their instruments. The horrific crash occurred within seconds just south of the little station at Grindstone, nearly nine miles north of Millinocket.

The excursion train got the worst of it. The tender "telescoped" the front end of the car, leaving five members of the band crushed to death and many injured. The dead were Frank Seely, Dr. Hugh Pipes, Harry Clark and Vergne Harris, all of Presque Isle, and Claude Loomer of Washburn. Also killed were Frank Garcelon of Houlton, the engineer, and one Gallagher, a fireman. George Estabrook of Linneus, brakeman, died later at Eastern Maine General Hospital in Bangor. The only death on the southbound train was H.F. Wentworth of Prospect, the fireman.

The death toll would have been worse if the trains had been going faster. Visibility was inhibited by the storm that swept eastern Maine that night, and by the fact that the track curved on the remote stretch where the accident occurred. Testimony at a hearing a few days later indicated the excursion train had slowed to about ten or twelve miles per hour, while the southbound train was moving at about twenty miles per hour.

Grindstone, population forty-three, was connected to the outer world by the railroad tracks and by a single telephone wire that was barely working because of the storm. "There was not even a logging road out of the hamlet, and, of course, no physicians or medical facilities," reported the *Bangor Daily Commercial* the afternoon after the wreck. The "husky lumbermen" employed there made quick work of "the shattered timbers and heavy piles of seats" trapping the dead and injured.

The only physician present, Dr. Ralph Foster of Brewer, had been a passenger on the southbound train. The only medical equipment he had was a hypodermic needle "which I afterwards used in relieving pain," he told a reporter. The injured were placed in a baggage car on seatbacks torn out of a passenger car. After awhile, the gaslights went out, and caregivers had to work by lantern light.

Other doctors began to arrive by train from Millinocket, Sherman, Houlton and, finally, Bangor. A cadre of nurses and physicians in Bangor had been notified of the disaster by Wingate Cram, son of the B&A's president, who spent much of the stormy evening riding about the Queen City in his open-top automobile summoning help.

The Railroad Commissioners of Maine and the Interstate Commerce Commission held a joint hearing on the cause of the wreck on August 2 in the Millinocket municipal courtroom up over the fire station. Their reports were unsparing in their condemnation of the excursion train's conductor, Herbert G. Dibble, and its late engineman, Frank Garcelon. An ICC report concluded that Dibble and Garcelon had tried to beat the southbound train, which had the right-of-way, to the Grindstone siding in violation of B&A speed rules and without sufficient time, especially considering the stormy conditions. After realizing the danger of collision just before the crash, Dibble could have stopped the train and taken safety precautions. Instead, he jumped off to safety.

The three members of the Maine Railroad Commission condemned the excursion train's "mad run" between Millinocket and Grindstone. They concluded, "The acts and conduct of Dibble and Garcelon were in violation of rules with which they were familiar, constituted a grossly reckless disregard of duty amounting to criminal carelessness and were the sole cause of the accident."

Dibble admitted responsibility for the wreck at the hearing. He admitted he did not figure out how much time was needed to get to the siding at Grindstone, relying on Garcelon's judgment instead. He admitted he had broken the rules in running by an earlier switch at Bowden's siding instead of pulling over to wait for the southbound regular to pass. He also admitted that he had disobeyed the rules by not stopping the train and sending out brakemen with lanterns and flares when he realized the danger just before meeting the southbound train.

The *Bangor Daily News* summed up the contents of his testimony in an August 3 headline: "CONDUCTOR DIBBLE TOOK A DESPERATE CHANCE AND LOST; Wreck Testimony Shows That Run From Millinocket Was a Gamble With Death."

A few months later, Dibble was sentenced to sixty days in jail and fined $500 after he pleaded guilty to a charge of manslaughter, according to both Bangor newspapers on February 14, 1912. The wreck cost the B&A more than $75,000 in claims and repairs, according to Jerry Angier and Herb Cleaves in their book *Bangor and Aroostook: The Maine Railroad.*

KILLER HEAT WAVE

July 11, 2011

Two months after Bangor's great fire of 1911, a terrific storm added to the destruction. A deadly heat wave roasted the city first. Thermometers rose well above 100 degrees in the shade. "BANGOR PEOPLE JUST BROILED ALIVE," proclaimed a headline in the *Bangor Daily News* on July 3 three days before the storm.

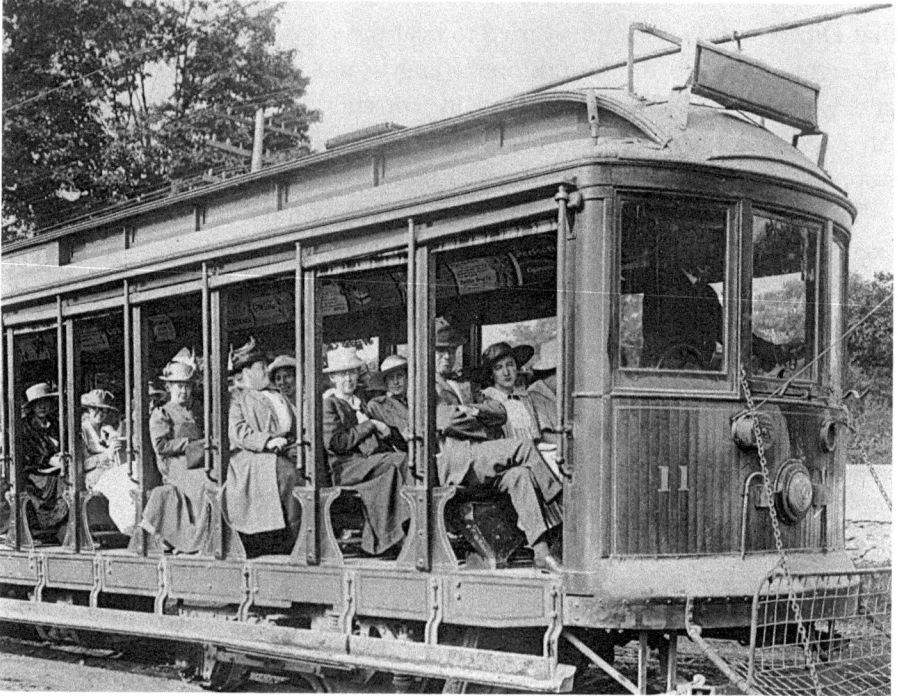

Bangor's open trolley cars proved a great way to keep cool during the heat wave of 1911. *Courtesy of Richard R. Shaw.*

Ice and electric fans were still luxuries for most people, and air conditioning was just a dream. Bangor did have open trolleys, however, in which people could enjoy the breeze. "From early morning until late at night, every car of the Bangor Railway and Electric Company both in and out of the city was jammed to the running boards," noted the newspaper a century ago this month.

The heat, along with the police, kept a lid on the usual Fourth of July hijinks. The city had banned torpedo canes, cannon crackers and blank revolvers, and the saloons were closed. "As a result, it was possible for most of the adult population to get some sleep," said the *Commercial*. Miraculously, no injuries from fireworks were reported, and drunken bullies were absent from the streets for a change.

A crowd of six thousand people "besieged" Riverside Park on the bank of the Penobscot River in Hampden at the end of the trolley line, taking full advantage of what little breeze was to be had. Black clouds rolled over the city. A little rain fell, but not enough to stop the heat.

Casualties from the heat were reported. City Engineer P.H. Coombs, one of the first affected, was overcome in his office, according to the *Bangor Daily Commercial* on July 3. He recovered at home. Many others collapsed in the days ahead.

The heat started killing people as the temperature ranged as high as 105 or 106 degrees in the shade on July 4. The first death was that of Martin Lawrence, about forty-five. He was found in a corridor at the Globe Hotel on French Street. No relatives were known. Lawrence had told people he had a home in Ireland.

Perhaps the heat would let up before the next big entertainment attraction. California Frank's Wild West Show was scheduled to perform on Thursday, July 6, at Maplewood Park (Bass Park). Buffalo Bill's famous show had appeared only a few weeks before, but Bangoreans seemed to have an unlimited appetite for western fantasies.

The morning of the show, the newspapers reported ominously that a "terrific thunderstorm"—a "near cyclone"—was moving up the Connecticut River valley. Meanwhile, Mrs. Myra Hudlin, sixty-nine, of 163 Third Street, collapsed "after having spent the morning over the wash tub." She died the next day. Identified in the *Commercial* as "a negress," Hudlin and her son had been burned out in the big fire on April 30. "There was nothing but a bed, six wooden chairs and a stove in the room where she died," reported the newspaper.

The storm hit at 2:30 p.m. A bold headline in the *Bangor Daily News* the next morning said, "BANGOR SWEPT UP BY GIGANTIC STORM... Five Days of Deadly Heat Followed by Fierce Cyclonic Disturbance Thursday Afternoon...ONE DEATH, MUCH RUIN IN ITS PATH... Almost a Panic as Circus Tents Collapse—Walls of Universalist Church Blown Down—Giant Trees Uprooted—Thousands of Dollars Worth of Property Destroyed."

Harry Norwood, a carpenter, died when a barn on the Pushaw Road collapsed on him. Frank Mower's dairy barn was one of several in the area destroyed by the wind.

Luckily, only a small crowd of about four hundred people had gathered to see California Frank. The tent consisted of an open arena in the center surrounded by seating for up to three thousand protected by an overhead canvas covering. When a section of this rig began to topple, the audience and performers fled into the arena, where they huddled as "debris hurled through the air" and the rain poured down on them.

Fay Ferrell, an eleven-year-old boy, nearly lost his ear when a pole fell on him and "he fell right in the path of the stampede." Others received cuts and bruises and a bad scare. Circus workers resurrected the tent, and that night, a better-attended show was held.

A great deal of property damage was done throughout the city. The east and west walls of the Universalist Church, a charred hulk from the recent fire perched over Center Park, came crashing down. The rear wall of the burned-out First Parish Church collapsed, as did the remains of some buildings on the east side of Exchange Street. Several layers of newly laid bricks were torn off a wall of the Jamieson building, under construction in East Market Square. Great sheets of copper were ripped from the top walls of the burned Post Office. "A heavy skylight from the YMCA building went cruising through the air," and "chimneys toppled in all directions."

Large plate-glass windows, a relative newcomer to Bangor's commercial building decor, were smashed in several stores, including a twelve-by-eight-foot pane at James A. Robinson & Co. on Hammond Street. Store awnings flew away, and large trees crashed into the streets. Electricity, trolley and telephone service went out just as they had after the fire, but not for long. Officials raced to repair damage.

How bad was this storm? The *Bangor Daily News* offered a homegrown assessment based on the memories of newsroom graybeards: "It was the greatest gale that Bangor had known since 1883, when the Court House was partially unroofed and the spire of the Universalist Church blown down, with the possible exception of that fierce blast that swept across the lower end of the city in 1890, causing the tragedy of the capsizing of the little steamer *Annie*."

The heat continued, part of the longest and hottest heat wave in New England history, according to David Ludlum (in 1976) in *The Country Journal New England Weather Book*. Hundreds died all over the Northeast. In Bangor, David Kerr, a waiter on the steamer *Belfast*, drowned while swimming at the ferry terminal late on the morning of July 10 with two other African American waiters. His death was attributed to the heat. Kerr complained of being exhausted and appeared to be dazed when thrown a line. Several other people, including Mrs. Stephen Bogrett, the wife of the manager of the Bijou Theater, were overcome that day. Another rainstorm hit late in the afternoon, but the heat returned.

Hundreds cooled off at their favorite swimming spots. These included the Brewer "sand bank" directly above the railroad bridge and the Bangor lumber docks, facing each other across the Penobscot River. The Prentiss boat house at the southerly end of the railroad bridge across the Kenduskeag, the beach at the lower end of the wharves down at High Head and two spots on the Kenduskeag known as "Sweet Home" and "The Stump" were other favorites, said the *Commercial* on July 12. The newspaper issued a warning that swimming under the bright sun at midday could bring on heat exhaustion and death.

On the morning of July 13, the *Bangor Daily News* issued a plaintive cry for relief. The big thermometer in front of Fowler's Pharmacy, on Main Street, had registered 101 degrees at 4:00 p.m. on Tuesday and 98 degrees at the same time on Wednesday. Downtown streets were deserted. Only one man in five was "punctilious enough" to wear a coat.

The crowds had abandoned the theaters by day but turned out at night "in various states of undress." West Market Square, the central boarding spot for the open-air trolleys, was jammed day and night by people desperately seeking a breeze. Some people, unable to flee to camps and summer cottages, slept on their porches and roofs.

"BANGOR STILL BROILS IN TROPICAL HEAT," the newspaper proclaimed, adding stoically, "No Use In Saying Much About it, But We Suffer Just The Same." The weather forecast said fair and slightly cooler.

GAS EXPLOSION ROCKED CITY

April 30, 2012

A huge explosion reverberated through downtown Bangor just after 3:00 p.m. on April 26, 1912, a century ago last week. A blast in an old brick reservoir under busy Mercantile Square left a crater thirty feet in diameter, unsealing a piece of the city's infrastructure that most people had forgotten existed.

"Showers of paving stones, with here and there solid blocks of granite, were hurled a dozen feet into the air, and clouds of

An underground reservoir filled with coal gas exploded in Mercantile Square in 1912. *Courtesy of Richard R. Shaw.*

dust for a few minutes blotted out the scene," recorded the *Bangor Daily News* the next morning.

A horse and wagon standing over the blast area were thrown ten feet into the air, falling back into the reservoir, which contained about six feet of water. A man who had started to walk across the square found himself standing at the edge of the pit when the dust cleared, miraculously unscathed by the flying debris.

Squares were located strategically around the city. These open commercial spaces, usually located at street intersections, allowed men driving horses and wagons to maneuver easily with their cargoes. Mercantile Square was one of four such spaces linked together running roughly parallel to Main Street and the Kenduskeag Stream. In order, they were West Market Square, Mercantile Square, Pickering Square and Hay Market Square.

Many of these spaces are gone today, and many of the buildings that stood around them have been torn down. West Market and Pickering still exist in attenuated versions along with their old names as public parks. Haymarket Square is a parking lot for Key Bank.

Mercantile Square was located in the general vicinity of what is today One Merchants Plaza and the Broad Street Market. It was one of the busiest spots in the city, "a favorite gathering place for baggage and furniture transfers, and at any hour of the day or evening the exact spot at which the explosion occurred has been covered with drivers, horses and wagons," said the *Bangor Daily News.*

Miraculously, at the time of the explosion, only the horse and wagon belonging to Charles B. Patterson, an expressman, was standing over the blast site. Patterson's son Carl was in charge of the wagon. Just before the concussion, he was standing nearby on the sidewalk near John T. Clark's clothing store at 33 Mercantile Square. He had been planning in a few seconds to walk into the square and climb onto the wagon.

The horse and the badly smashed wagon landed in the reservoir about five feet below the surface of the street. Men rushed forward into the opening with ropes and a plank. They helped the "snorting, struggling animal" climb out of the hole nearly unscathed, and they brought out the wagon in pieces.

Meanwhile, frightened by the noise, "nearly a dozen horses started up Broad Street on the run and almost a like number headed toward Pickering square and down Broad Street. They were stopped by the police and bystanders without damage in each instance," reported the *Bangor Daily Commercial* the next afternoon.

The fire department spent nearly half an hour pumping an estimated ten thousand gallons of water from the pit. Only then were officials sure no one had been killed.

The reservoir was part of a system of underground water storage areas built over the years all over the city for fighting fires. Both newspapers agreed that this particular one was built in 1865.

The *Bangor Daily News* said these reservoirs were "mostly forgotten and long unused." The newspaper said the building of the city's waterworks on the Penobscot River in 1875 "made them no longer necessary."

The *Commercial* reported, however, that this particular reservoir had been used as recently as the fire that destroyed much of the downtown a year ago. Indeed, both the fire and police chiefs said it should be restored.

The big question was what had caused the blast. Everyone seemed to agree that gas had accumulated in the hole and exploded. But was it sewer gas or illuminating gas? The latter was produced by burning coal at the Bangor Gaslight Company on Main Street. This coal gas was used by people to light their homes and to power small stoves and water heaters. Underground gas lines ran throughout the city. "I am very certain it was not illuminating gas," C.R. Stull, general manager of the gaslight company, told the *Bangor Daily News* for the first day story. "We have two mains in the vicinity—one 20 feet from the reservoir and the other 50 feet. There was no leak from either. I am quite positive because workmen had been testing them a few hours before."

City officials were skeptical of Stull's claims. "Illuminating gas was the cause of the explosion," stated Fire Chief Mason. "I am very sure because when we arrived, fire was coming out around the sides [of the hole]." Many people who worked in the area had smelled the gas. Indeed, gas company employees had been there trying to discover if there was such a leak.

Hearings before the city's public utilities committee revealed a recent history of gas odors and testing for leaks in the area. For example, Henry C. Bean, an expressman "who stands on Mercantile Square, told of having seen two men digging in front of Fred Crowell's produce establishment [at 47 Pickering Square] about 11 o'clock on the morning of the explosion. He said one of the men struck a match and flames spurted out of the hole." The workmen were unable to find a leak, however. Other witnesses told of the strong smell of gas in their stores and in the air a day or two before the explosion.

A University of Maine chemistry professor, Ralph H. McKee, was hired to conduct tests. One of his samples, taken from a hole in the pavement in front of Thurston & Kingsbury's at 68 Broad Street, contained enough illuminating gas to explode violently when mixed with air and ignited. Other samples showed no gas.

The public utilities committee had heard enough. They concluded in May that responsibility for the blast lay with the gaslight company. The next step was to take up negotiations with the company about payment to repair the reservoir and the square.

Chapter 4

The Great Fire of 1911

Small Fires Plagued City

April 18, 2011

In the days immediately before the great fire that destroyed much of downtown Bangor on Sunday, April 30, 1911, residents of the Queen City of the East found many worrisome stories to ponder in their daily newspapers. Fires on Friday, for example, caused major destruction in three Maine towns, destroying large sawmills in Fairfield; ten buildings, including the town hall, in Harrington; and eleven dwellings in Livermore Falls, leaving eighteen families homeless. Dry conditions throughout the state aggravated these fires and many smaller ones.

Bangor was experiencing a run of minor fires. They were reported in the newspapers on an almost daily basis during the week before the big fire.

On April 25, small blazes were extinguished at the Third Street dump and in a dock shed at the Maine Central freight yard on Hancock Street.

Two days later, the newspapers reported five minor fires kept firemen busy—a chimney blaze at Mrs. N.H. Bragg's residence on Third Street, a woods fire on Olive Street, a grass fire set by some youngsters behind Parker Street, and two dump fires, one at the Bangor Railway and Electric Company's car barn on Main Street and the other on Fern Street.

The next day, three more fires were reported—a chimney fire at Timothy Sullivan's at 143 Lincoln Street, a pile of new poles ablaze in back of the

Dazed onlookers walked the streets in Bangor's burned district the morning after the great fire of 1911. Much of the city's downtown area had been destroyed. *Courtesy of Richard R. Shaw.*

BR&E Co.'s car barn and a grass fire at a farm on Fuller Road. The next day was nearly a repeat, as a barn at 48 Webster Avenue was set on fire by hot ashes and the tower on the Hammond Street Congregational Church scorched by hot solder being used for repairs.

Fire Chief William Mason threatened to prosecute anyone setting fires near buildings or dry brush, the *Bangor Daily News* reported on April 29. The night before, boys had set two small fires, one in a pile of boughs pressed up against a summer house at 163 Broadway and another in grass behind a barn on Essex Street. Chief Mason's press interview was cut short by an alarm for a dump fire on Pier Street.

I recite these relatively trivial events to give readers an idea of all the possible sources of incineration a century ago in a city littered with fire hazards. To what extent the average Bangorean may have been worried, it's hard to tell. City residents had been warned many times by the fire chief and the newspapers. However, chances are people were interested in events more tangible than an imaginary fire.

The entertainment scene was lively at the city's theaters. Topping the bill on the night before the great fire was "Gentleman Jim" Corbett, the former heavyweight boxing champ, at the Bangor Opera House. The personable pugilist, who had defeated John L. Sullivan many years before for the championship, had entered vaudeville. He was appearing as "interlocutor and monologist" with George Evans's Honey Boy Minstrels. "When asked the usual question about the 'White Man's Hope,' as far as he could see the white man just at the present time hasn't any hope," reported the *Bangor Daily Commercial* reporter, referring to the concerns of many whites that a black man, Jack Johnson, held the boxing crown.

Sports fans had other exciting things to ponder as well besides small fires. An item in the *Bangor Daily News* that morning was proposing a marathon from Old Town to Bangor on Memorial Day featuring Andrew Sockalexis, the new running sensation from Indian Island who had performed so well recently in the Boston Marathon.

There were so many other diversions to think about as well. The Bijou Theater was being completely redesigned and expanded to house a better class of vaudeville; a Style Show—like the Food Show and the Auto Show that had been held recently—was being planned at City Hall in May so Bangor merchants could show off the latest fashions; the Bangor Yacht Club had held a smoker Friday night at its clubhouse below the Tin Bridge near the Hampden line; and the ice was going out on Phillips Lake—good news for fishermen.

Spring was definitely in the air along with the smell of smoke. A fashion milestone had been reached only yesterday. "The first straw hat of the season was seen on the street Friday afternoon, and the wearer seemed unaware of his distinction. The ice having now been broken, the lightweight lids will soon predominate," reported the *Bangor Daily News* that Saturday afternoon before the great fire.

Amidst all these lighthearted news items, however, was one whose ominous significance could not possibly have been understood by even the most perceptive readers. The first schooner of the season after ice left the Kenduskeag Stream had been seen moving into the stream from the Penobscot River through the railroad drawbridge, the *Commercial* reported on April 21. The two-masted *G. Stancliff* was carrying a load of goods from Boston to J. Frank Green, who had a warehouse on Broad Street, beside the stream. The load included "paper, pitch, hardware, and miscellaneous merchandise."

Green's shed on Broad Street, where he stored hay and tar paper, was where the conflagration started. We can guess today that the *G. Stancliff* was carrying some of the fuel that contributed to Bangor's disaster a few days later.

LEGENDS OF THE GREAT FIRE

May 2, 2011

Legends of Bangor's fire of Sunday, April 30, 1911, began circulating through the city before firemen had put out the flames that destroyed fifty-five acres, more than one hundred businesses, the public library, the post office, the high school, seven churches and nearly three hundred residences. Here are a few of the tales that attracted my attention as I read the century-old newspaper accounts appearing the week after the conflagration.

Two men, John Scribner and George Abbott, both of Brewer, died, and many more people had close calls. For example, Frank C. Hinckley became trapped by flames on the roof of the Episcopal church. He escaped by sliding down the belfry rope. Jacob Tertzaz, a University of Maine law student, broke his foot when he jumped out of a second-floor window after trying to save books in the school library, then located on Exchange Street. Tertzaz and other students who also jumped from the burning building covered their heads with blankets to avoid breathing the smoke.

Stories like these were repeated over and over in the newspapers. Some sound like urban myths today. In one, a baby carriage catches fire from falling embers while the nameless father or mother is busy watching the city burn. The baby is rescued in the nick of time. I read at least three variations of this story.

Tales of pathos were common. A girl wept in front of the burned-out high school because she would not be able to graduate. An old woman clutched two quilts and her pet dog, recounting how she had just made the last payment on her burned house and she had no insurance.

Incidents of valiant resistance abounded as well. "Operators, all girls, of the telephone exchange, stuck courageously to their posts and answered calls until the police by main force had to drag them from their switchboard. A few fainted, in all, the act being one of great heroism," reported the *Bangor Daily News* on the Monday morning after the fire.

While the greatest heroes were the city's overwhelmed firemen, there were many incidents of workers or neighbors pitching in to save buildings or whole neighborhoods. "The Graphic Theater and the Burns building on the other side of York Street was saved by theater employees using garden hose and buckets," reported the *Bangor Daily News*.

Sometimes, women whose husbands were busy fighting the fire downtown were the principal actors. Out on Essex Street, "one squad of women,

Residents who had lived in the heart of the fire district had to guard their belongings until they could have them moved away. *Courtesy of Richard R. Shaw.*

The Bass building "firewall" that blocked the fire from continuing on to City Hall. *Courtesy of Richard R. Shaw.*

Mrs. Hattie Jordan, Mrs. Millicent B. Adams, Mrs. George Francis and Mrs. Rockwell G. Youngs...successfully prevented many fires from gaining headway," recounted the *Bangor Daily Commercial* on May 6.

One of the most important deterrents to the flames was a "firewall." The thick brick wall on the north end of the Bass block at Franklin and Hammond Streets was credited with stopping the fire before it crossed Hammond and destroyed City Hall and possibly far more, according to the *Bangor Daily Commercial* on May 1.

By day, the city was besieged by sightseers who came on special excursion trains armed with cameras. They were restrained by 450 "specials"—police, militia, college cadets and Boy Scouts who patrolled the ruins.

"Swarms of professional beggars" appeared outside the fire district. They went door to door "showing fantastically bandaged limbs" claiming they had been injured in the fire, the *Bangor Daily News* noted on May 5. Looters in the burned district, however, were relatively scarce, probably thanks to the "specials."

A strange silence pervaded the city at night. In the burned district, chimneys rose starkly in the air like tombstones by moonlight. Burning piles of coal smoldered in the gaping holes in the ground that had been basements.

Sometimes, a building appeared whole but was really just an empty hulk. In one such fire-gutted French Street mansion, with walls and roof still standing, this glowing mass of coal in the basement cast a ghoulish light through gaping windows and doors as if a party was on, recorded a reporter from the *Bangor Daily News* out for a late-night stroll on May 2.

The play at the Bangor Opera House attracted a large crowd the night after the fire even though the scenery and actors were veiled in gaslit shadows due to the electricity being disconnected. Outside, after the show, the audience was greeted by blackest night, and young ladies were said to be happy to be accompanied home by male escorts. The streets were illuminated only in the burned district, where fires still smoldered.

A large relief effort was mounted. More than $50,000 was collected locally. Donations from other cities arrived as well. Boston sent fifty iron beds with bedding.

How many people actually needed aid? Estimates of the number of homeless families published in the newspapers ranged from seventy-five to three hundred. The number of "destitute" families, however, was another matter, and efforts were made as usual to separate the "deserving" poor from the "undeserving" poor.

Some people refused to take aid out of principle, noted the papers. Jokes were made about a few applicants who demanded cigarettes or who scornfully rejected used clothing. One woman reportedly demanded money to pay the doctor who treated her after she sprained her ankle running to see the fire.

But there was "very little suffering," concluded the *Commercial*. Many of the homeless were helped by friends and relatives. Many still had jobs. The newspaper contained numerous announcements of businesses that moved from their burned-out headquarters to new office spaces outside the fire zone.

People could apply for temporary aid and jobs at the Chamber of Commerce at City Hall. The ever-enthusiastic Jennie Johnson, the city missionary, fell down some stairs there Monday night, spraining her ankle, but continued to stand on crutches at a table at the entrance "handing out cheer and aid to the needy," said the *Bangor Daily News* on May 3.

Private groups helped out as well. The local chapter of the Red Cross set up stations on the East Side at the home of the Reverend Alva R. Scott and on the West Side "in the billiard room at the residence of Mrs. E.R. Burpee." Prominent society women dispensed donated clothing, noted the *Commercial* on May 6.

The Salvation Army was burned out of its headquarters, but energetic Adjutant Armstrong hired a horse and wagon and was distributing donated clothing, bedding and other supplies, reported the *Bangor Daily News* on May 6.

Meanwhile, Bangoreans maintained their sense of "humor and carelessness to discomfort." This anonymous conversation, purported to have been overheard by a *Bangor Daily News* writer, appeared in the paper on May 4.

"Hello Joe. How did you make out?"

"Well, my house burned."

"Save anything?"

"No."

"Any insurance?"

"Not a cent."

"Well, anyway, you've got a job."

"Nope—place of business burned out."

"Come in—let's talk it over."

"Can't stop now, old man—I'm going to the theater."

Yes, it takes a lot to keep Bangor people away from a Broadway show, noted the newsman.

CITY FOUGHT TO RESTORE UTILITIES

May 16, 2011

Bangoreans were proud of their public utilities, and they watched with horror when the conflagration of Sunday, April 30, 1911, shut them down one by one. Electricity, gas, telephones, clean water—all failed, canceling temporarily the progress that had been achieved in the Queen City of the East during the last few decades. Many Bangoreans could remember the days before any of these luxuries existed. Their availability marked the difference between a "queen city" and a backwoods town where wood stoves and outhouses still reigned.

One of the most damaging blows was the destruction of the Bangor Railway & Electric Company's Park Street substation. It put out the incandescent lights (fifty-six thousand bulbs in use, the *Industrial Journal* had reported the year before) in homes and businesses in the area and stopped the trolley cars in their tracks. (The city's municipal electrical generating system, which powered street lights and lights in public buildings, also failed.) "The rotary converters and the lighting transformers were absolutely ruined, and the storage batteries valued at $25,000 were also rendered useless for all time. The transmission lines were burned out as far as Broadway and Garland Streets," Clarence Tolman, chief electric engineer for the BR&E Co. told the *Bangor Daily Commercial* on Monday, May 1.

Many people depended on the electric cars to get to work. The tracks wound through Bangor's streets and connected several smaller towns to the metropolis. Across the Penobscot River, the Brewer cars were also out of service—nor were they running out to Kenduskeag, East Corinth and Charleston. Down in Hampden, Henry Mayo's automobile was placed at the disposal of local people who depended on the trolley. Only the cars to Old Town continued operating (above the Bangor dam), because they were powered by a generating plant in Veazie.

The Bangor Gaslight Company, which serviced more than 3,300 meters, was also affected. Gas produced by burning coal was used for lighting and cooking. People living on the city's West Side—west of the Kenduskeag Stream—were still cooking with gas, but not those on the East Side, where the fire concentrated. The company told the newspaper it expected to have the East Side fixed by Wednesday.

The area's more than four thousand telephone subscribers lost service as well. The New England Telephone and Telegraph Company's office on Exchange Street had been incinerated. The "hello girls" were ordered out of the building by police as they made a heroic stand at the switchboard. While their male supervisors stood by with fire extinguishers, the police hurried the ladies from the room. Some reportedly fainted in the smoke. A new switchboard was ordered from Boston. Long-distance calls were still possible through a network of temporary connections.

Meanwhile, the Postal Telegraph Service stayed open. The manager and two operators "deserve great credit for sticking to their instruments when the flames were raging in the rear of the office" in the Bass building at Franklin and Hammond Streets behind a brick firewall that blocked the inferno. Messenger boys volunteered for duty during the night, and extra operators came up from Portland and Waterville. The city's other telegraph companies were also able to stay open.

When people thought things couldn't get any worse, this headline appeared in the *Commercial* on Tuesday, May 2: "DON'T DRINK CITY WATER." Water had been pumped directly from the polluted river into the mains without treatment so the fire department would have enough to

The State Street loop trolley, which ran between the Penobscot Exchange on Exchange Street to Cumberland and French Streets, was the first to get going after the fire. *Courtesy of Richard R. Shaw.*

fight the flames. If one wanted to avoid typhoid fever and other illnesses, he should get his water elsewhere.

As the days went by, the trolley system was gradually reassembled. The first local car got underway Tuesday, May 2, on the State Street loop, running between the Penobscot Exchange hotel on Exchange Street to Cumberland and French Streets. The rest of the system would not be working for several days.

In all, "approximately two miles of trolley wire, several times as much more guy wire and over 200 poles" were destroyed on the city's East Side. A crew of fifty men employed by the BR&E Co. had been cleaning up the debris and barking and peeling new poles at the company's High Head plant, reported the *Commercial* on Friday, May 5.

The next day, power was restored throughout the city. The BR&E Co. had completed building two temporary electrical generating stations on Franklin and Garland Streets, said the *Commercial*. The newspaper story gave a blow-by-blow account of the breakneck effort to get the proper parts from the General Electric Company in Schenectady, New York, by train to Bangor and then assembled and running. Just after noon, the entire streetcar system was running on its old schedule.

Meanwhile, city government officials had succeeded in restoring streetlights, lighting in municipal buildings and fire alarms. The streetlights were back on Wednesday night, May 3, and the last part of the system, the police signal network, was expected to be working Saturday night. All that was left now was to get the phones working and clean drinking water flowing, but that would take another week.

The telephone system was up and working at 5:55 p.m. Friday, May 12, the *Commercial* announced the next day. The phone company's new office was in the Bass building facing Hammond Street, the building with the famous firewall that had been credited with saving City Hall and perhaps much of the rest of the West Side from destruction. The *Commercial* continued:

> *Sighs of relief went up all over the city Friday night at the resumption of the telephone service. For 13 days, Bangor has been without them, and people have come to appreciate their convenience as never before. Business houses especially have been greatly hampered. Matters which usually could be adjusted by a two-minute telephone talk have sometimes taken hours— hours of time and an infinite amount of running about. Housewives have been greatly troubled by their inability to order meats and groceries, and daily trips to the markets have been necessitated. In many instances, the markets and grocery stores have sent their teams to regular customers each morning when the orders for the day have been taken.*

"WATER IS SAFE AGAIN," announced a story in the same newspaper. The mains and "dead ends" had been flushed out and the water analyzed. "Not a drop of river water that was pumped directly into the water mains during the big fire remains, so complete was the flushing." Of course, many people had not trusted the purity of the city's water supply even before the fire.

If people wished to escape these inconveniences, they could hop aboard a train or steamboat and go someplace else. The city's two major transportation routes were still open for business. Or, as is clear from several newspaper reports, some people went on fishing trips to their camps as ice left the ponds in the area.

"STRONG MEN" SEIZED THE DAY

June 13, 2011

The Reverend David Beach, president of Bangor Theological Seminary. *Courtesy of Richard R. Shaw.*

The conventional wisdom is that the fire was an unmitigated disaster for the Queen City of the East. Yet many of Bangor's leaders saw immediately something quite different as they surveyed the smoking ruins. Amidst the wreckage, they envisioned a historic opportunity to transform the city into a place more closely approximating its regal nickname.

That Monday morning, the day after the fire, David Beach, president of Bangor Theological Seminary, wrote in the *Bangor Daily News* that he saw "a silver lining" in the disaster. "In this moment of appalling calamity, Bangor faces the future with undaunted spirit. The enterprise and taste which have built the city will swiftly rebuild its burned section," wrote the Reverend Beach, one of the city's most respected civic leaders. "As with Chicago, Boston, Baltimore, Portland and other cities which have experienced like disasters, the rebuilding will be more substantial, convenient and imposing." Beach predicted Bangor would be "the busiest city in Maine for a long time to come" thanks to the building boom ahead. That meant lots of jobs with good wages—something Bangoreans valued far more than old buildings, many of which had been falling down.

The *Bangor Daily Commercial*, the city's other newspaper, offered its readers a similar vision on May 3. Robert Sprague, a University of Maine economics

Several local architects survey the fire scene. *Courtesy of Richard R. Shaw.*

and sociology professor and a well-known progressive commentator, wrote, "Bangor today has the greatest opportunity to become really the Queen City of the East, the most beautiful town on the coast." He called upon the city's "strong men" to step forth and shape the community's destiny. "I have never known a city to have such a natural opportunity [to become] a great civic center which would be a glory to her forever."

But what could anyone do? Hadn't the city received a serious financial blow, perhaps a deathblow? Not by a long shot, the *Bangor Daily News* pointed out confidently May 3 in its lead news story:

> *Bangor is rich and can well restore what has been lost. There is ample capital here, and there will be two millions in insurance. The circumstances that created Bangor, the resources that gave prosperity and growth to the city, still exist, and the enterprise of Bangoreans is not to be discouraged or their activities halted by disasters like that of Sunday.*

Very little of the city's industrial capacity or its transportation infrastructure had been destroyed. Businesses in the burned-out district were moving quickly into temporary quarters. As long as trees grew in the woods, and lumber barons and other entrepreneurs had big bank accounts and ample insurance policies, Bangor's future looked bright to thinking people.

On May 2, about six hundred of Bangor's "strong men" assembled at City Hall to discuss what could be done. One of the city's economic leaders, John R. Graham, president of the Bangor Railway & Electric Company, offered inspiring testimony about his own plans: "I started this afternoon on my building [excavation had begun before the fire]…only instead of making it five stories, I'm going to make it six." (The John R. Graham building still sits at the corner of Central and Harlow Streets, a monument to Bangor's post-fire spirit.)

Graham said he had also hired an architect to draw up plans for his new home on French Street, which had also burned. He pledged $1,000 of his own money and $1,000 of his company's for the city's relief fund. "The hall rang with applause," recorded the *Bangor Daily News*. Graham continued, "It may sound cruel to say in the face of this great calamity that it is a good thing for Bangor…[but] I think we are to have a bigger, a better, and a busier Bangor before we get through." Graham said he had begun buying up property in the burned-out district where he planned to erect more buildings. He said he had borrowed $200,000 toward that end.

The next day, May 3, Patrick T. Dugan, manufacturer of trunks, bags and cases and dealer in harnesses and saddles, became the first person to apply for a permit to build in the burned section of the city. His plans called for a three- or four-story brick building at 32 Central Street, his previous place of business. On May 13, the *Commercial* reported that the first house in Bangor's burned section had been framed by contractor A.M. Taylor at 86 Center Street for the Daley family.

By Friday, May 5, the *Bangor Daily News* was able to declare, "It is becoming more and more apparent that Bangor's great fire was for the city as a whole a blessing in disguise. This summer and next will see the city's burned district rebuilt with a rapidity equaling that of any boom town in the west." The story contained a long list of speculative plans on the part of property owners who said they would be rebuilding with stone and brick under proposed regulations (passed by the city council on May 9). Many old wooden buildings, which had been firetraps and eyesores, had been destroyed in the fire.

By Saturday, May 6, one week after the fire, the newspaper was able to declare confidently in its lead headline, "KENDUSKEAG PARKWAY TO BEAUTIFY BANGOR." That was an early reference to what would develop over the decades into the greenway (and fire break) along the banks of the Kenduskeag Stream from the Penobscot River to the former locations of the U.S. Post Office and Customs House and Norombega Hall, which had been located in the stream between State and Franklin Streets. A few days later, it was announced that Edward Blake and Mrs. Charles Wood had donated land for the project.

A committee, consisting of City Engineer Philip Coombs, John Frawley, the drugstore owner, and Franklin Bragg of N.H. Bragg & Sons, had been appointed to consider this and other proposals for rearranging the downtown area. Boston landscape designer Warren H. Manning was hired a few days later to draw up a plan.

Within one week of the fire, the groundwork had been laid for building a new Bangor downtown. There would be heated arguments over some of the ideas. Not everyone would get what he wanted. Nevertheless, the Queen City of the East would get back on its feet, a bigger city than before.

Now it was time to relax a little. Bangor's first movie theater, the Nickel, was back in business on Friday, May 5. After its Central Street building burned, it had moved quickly to the old Acker's Theater building on Union Street. The seats were filled on re-opening night, and films included *The Phony Prince* and *The White Squaw*, which featured "the original Deadwood stagecoach." Of course, local talent performed the usual illustrated songs. "It is time now to seek a little wholesome recreation after the strain and terrors of the week," declared the *Bangor Daily News*.

Shack Stores Grew Like Mushrooms

June 27, 2011

Immediately after the fire, businessmen scurried about looking for places to set up shop so they could start making money again. The city council allowed them to build temporary wooden structures along the streets in the fire district. Center Park, located where City Hall sits today, was thrown open to mercantile squatters as well. These "shack stores" could be no more than fourteen feet high and were supposed to be removed by January 1, 1912.

"Shacks sprung up like mushrooms until the upper East Side section [of the city] looked like a mining camp," noted the *Bangor Daily News* on July 1, 1911, two months after the fire. "The shacks were built as cheaply as possible

Businessmen built shacks along several streets until proper buildings could be constructed. *Courtesy of Richard R. Shaw.*

and covered with roofing paper. They cost from $25 to $1,500." Some of these shacks were built on the spot where their owners had done business before the fire. Several businesses moved to Center Park. Many shacks were a joint venture on the part of two or more proprietors. Appropriate notices were posted in the city's newspapers.

The first concern to open for business was M. Schwartz Sons, which manufactured saws and sold mill supplies. They "built a commodious shack facing French Street, in the rear of their lot which was numbered 213 Exchange Street." A "slight accident" to the building occurred, however, when a portion of the ruins of the back wall of the seven-story Morse-Oliver building at the corner of State and Exchange Streets was dynamited. Part of the wreckage fell on Schwartz's new headquarters through a "slight miscalculation." A benefit of these shacks was that they were easy to build and repair, and the damage was fixed in a few hours, according to the newspaper.

The Maine Woolen Company; the Abel Hunt Estate, casket manufacturer and undertaker; and M. Lynch, locksmith, joined in erecting a store on the east side of East Market Square (the intersection of Harlow and Park Streets in front of Center Park). It was on the site of the burned-out Granite Block, "a row of ancient granite buildings," where their businesses had been located previously.

P.T. Dugan & Co., which had manufactured harnesses and trunks at a Central Street location, and marketmen D. H. & I.E. Collins, who had operated on Exchange Street, built shacks on prominent locations in Center Park.

On the Park Street side of the park a row of carpenters' and painters' shacks sprouted. G. McKenney, E.R. Brooks, K.J. Anderson, H.W. Matthews and W.W. Frost did business on "the Park street mall."

John R. Graham, one of Bangor's most prominent property owners, built a solid structure for three of his tenants who had done business in his former building on Central Street. They were the Grand Union Tea Company; Carl S. Preble, druggist; and the Rice & Tyler music store. Graham, who was president of the Bangor Railway and Electric Company, did things with flair. He hired the Bangor Band to play a concert from the roof of the new building.

Just south of there were shacks occupied by contractors Flanders & Son and A.B. Newcomb, Lane's shoe shop, an unnamed barber shop, the Troy Laundry and harness-maker Edward Jordan. Otto Nelson, the contractor, was also nearby.

The largest shack store was that of Brown & White, manufacturer of carriages and sleighs, located on the west side of East Market Square. Used primarily as a showroom, this shack also rented space to a fish market.

Many other shack stores were scattered through the burned district. The Bangor Railway and Electric Company's new transformer station on Garland Street, which powered the city's trolley system as well as much of its electric lighting, was put up in two days. The city had erected two "shack fire stations" in Abbot Square, where the high school had burned, across Harlow Street from where the Bangor Public Library is today.

How many of these "shack dwellers" would still be there come January 1? Given the intensity of the debate over a new plan for downtown and the pace of reconstructing permanent buildings, probably quite a few.

Meanwhile, an editorial entitled "DESOLATION," on June 28, described a far different scene along burned-out sections of French Street and Broadway, where fine houses belonging to Bangor's wealthier folks had stood. No shacks were going up there. The editorial writer said a walk through that area was like a visit to the west coast of Ireland, where the crumbling ruins of old castles still stood "clad in clinging ivy."

Likewise, this wasteland, where big houses had once stood, was anything but barren. The writer noted:

In Bangor, the sweet peas, planted before the great incineration, are up and thriving nearby, a foot high. The blackened chimneys stand out, bare and forbidding, as if a host of hostile invaders had been along, with spears and blazing torches. There are modern pansies and gaudy peonies in bloom by the sides of brick heaps. Tiger lilies spring flauntingly above the brick and concrete walks and under the scorched trees, where glad children frolicked and screamed a year ago are warted toads and slimy snails.

Save for the occasional "artillery-like explosions"—dynamite blasts and collapsing walls—heard early every morning and the rumbling carts taking away broken bricks and mortar, "there is little to remind one that the Bangor that was known and beloved a year ago will be resurrected from the ashes within another year," this newspaper editorial writer predicted optimistically. As sure as the shack stores had sprung up down the hill and the spring flowers had pushed through the ashes on Broadway, he was right.

City Swapped Park for New Post Office

October 31, 2011

The era of political good feeling that followed the fire ended abruptly on May 25 with an editorial blast condemning the recommendations of the committee appointed to restore and beautify the burned area. "Jules Verne in his palmiest days never evolved a more ridiculous or impracticable plan," harangued the *Bangor Daily Commercial*. The newspaper's main objection sounds familiar today. The proposed changes "would mortgage Bangor's future for generations to come and saddle the city with a debt from which it would never emerge."

In the months ahead, a series of battles occurred over the locations for a new library, high school, central fire station and other public buildings burned in the fire, as well as over the widening of Central Street and other proposals. J.P. Bass, publisher of the *Commercial*, and other fiscal conservatives squared off against powerful progressives like John R. Graham, head of the trolley company. Personal attacks based on decades-old animosities surfaced in both of the city's newspapers, with the *Bangor Daily News* backing the advocates of expensive improvements against the shrill and relentlessly negative *Commercial*.

Center (or Central) Park as it appeared in front of the First Universalist Church before the fire. The bandstand can be seen through the trees. Bangor's new post office replaced most of the park. *Courtesy of Richard R. Shaw.*

The new post office was erected after the fire where Center Park had been, directly in front of the First Universalist Church. *Courtesy of Richard R. Shaw.*

One of these battles interested me more than the others because of the clash of cultures it represented. That was the decision by city fathers to sacrifice a popular downtown park for a new post office. This new post office was eventually converted into today's Bangor City Hall.

The old U.S. Customs House and Post Office, which had stood in the Kenduskeag Stream between State and Central Streets where Kenduskeag Parkway Mall is today, burned in the fire. In a plan worked out with the federal government, city planners wanted to have a new post office in Center (or Centre or even Central) Park, which was bounded by Park, Harlow and Center (or Centre) Streets.

Center Park, which sat on a grassy slope in front of the Universalist Church, occupied a special place in the minds of many Bangoreans. The Bangor Band had played in its bandstand (situated about where City Hall steps are located today), and famous people like James G. Blaine had delivered speeches there.

The park was near a rough, working-class neighborhood. An effort to make it the site of a new public library had failed in 1905. The major argument against the idea resurfaced six years later: Center Park was the only nearby green space for the numerous poor who lived in the area. "That's a breathing place for the poor people of the city and where they don't have their own lawns to sit out on it seems a shame to cut them out of the park," Bangor resident Frank J. Cluff told a *Commercial* reporter on July 27.

On September 28, a deal won the approval of city officials. "THE CITY CLINCHES SPLENDID BARGAIN," cheered the *Bangor Daily News* the next morning. The federal government would give the city $100,000 (plus the old post office site in the Kenduskeag) for the park. The only opponents were an alderman and four councilors. (The federal government approved the plan in November.)

The *Commercial* complained even louder. The city had approved the deal, "ignoring a strong appeal in behalf of the people, who for 50 years and over have owned and enjoyed the privileges of Centre Park," said the lead on its story that afternoon. An editorial the next day excoriated city fathers. The "very improper action" was the result of a "wicked proposition," indeed "a monstrous proposition," which did not represent the true sentiments of the people. The high cost of post-fire renovations had influenced the vote. In other words, officials were willing to sell the popular park to reduce the city's debt. It was the "height of absurdity to take one of the few beauty spots of the city…and use it for a granite building under the guise of civic improvement."

Meanwhile, the rebuilding of the city progressed steadily. A temporary post office was placed on Central Street in a building rapidly erected by John R. Graham on the site where the Nickel Theater had sat before the fire. The street was buzzing with construction, and the temporary post office was "HARD TO GET TO" because of all the work going on, complained a headline in the *Bangor Daily News* on October 6. The newspaper's description gives a good idea of what it was like to walk through the burned-over part of the downtown:

> *If one goes over Harlow Street, beginning at the East Side corner, he first encounters piles of bricks and timber and mud, derricks and so on; then he runs into a lunch wagon, then comes a sea of mud, then a few yards of the old sidewalk, then more mud, then more of the debris of building operations. On either side of Central Street, down to the* [temporary] *Post Office, it is the same, and the foot passenger must take the middle of the road. In front of the Post Office is a nice new cement sidewalk, but going west, toward Hammond Street, it is mud and hurdles of wreckage and more mud and more debris.*

Thus, Bangor was reconstructed brick by board, with sound and fury nearly every step of the way, as well as lots of mud and wreckage. Today, we can only wonder how J.P. Bass would react to the great changes going on in the park that bears his name uptown at Main and Buck Streets—the site of a huge new city arena. But we can make an educated guess.

Trade Triumphed

January 23, 2012

Bangor rapidly rose from the ashes in the months after the fire. By October, forty new houses were either completed or being built. By December, the Bangor and Aroostook Railroad and some other tenants were mostly moved into the new six-story Graham Building at Harlow and Central Streets. On January 13, 1912, one of the city's finest hotels, the Windsor ("All rooms have running hot and cold water and 40 have baths."), reopened nearby. A few days later, the *Bangor Daily News* printed a picture of the new Largay, Adams and Bangor Cigar Manufacturing Co.'s new

Above: The new Windsor Hotel, with shops for local businesses at street level, was one of the signs that Bangor was returning to economic vitality after the fire. *Courtesy of Richard R. Shaw.*

Left: The new John R. Graham Building became central office space for the Bangor and Aroostook Railroad and the Bangor Railway and Electric Company. *Courtesy of Richard R. Shaw.*

buildings on State Street, which had been "completed and occupied less than eight months after the fire."

Construction was rampant throughout the burned district. In some spots downtown, streets and sidewalks were almost impossible to navigate, raising the ire of the *Bangor Daily News*. A new high school, a public library, a new post office and dozens more houses, office buildings and municipal structures were under construction or on the drawing board. The pace was so fast that some fiscal conservatives, like the publisher of the *Bangor Daily Commercial*, complained the city would go into debt forever. Where was all the money coming from? Newspapers had been lamenting the decline of the city's legendary lumber industry and the stagnation of its harbor for years. The city's manufacturing output was modest—some footwear, stoves, trunks and wood products. Yet the *Bangor Daily News* boasted just days after the fire that "Bangor is rich and can well restore what it has lost." Men who had been making lots of money were not about to abandon the Queen City of the East.

In fact, Bangoreans were getting richer. The city was growing. The *Commercial* explained a major reason for the city's increasing wealth on January 6, 1912. Bangor was a rapidly growing wholesale center for a vast region, which, until recently, had consisted mainly of empty wilderness. In the vernacular of the time, the "backbone" of the city's business life was the "jobbing trade."

While "jobbing houses" had always been an important part of the city's economy, the wholesale business now had emerged as its lifeblood thanks to the rise of railroads, and one railroad in particular—the Bangor and Aroostook—during the past few decades. The days were over when Bangor merchants rented schooners to haul their products to down-east ports. And much of Aroostook County's rich agricultural land was also open for business thanks to the B&A.

Bangor was "the shipping center of a lumber and agriculture empire," noted the *Commercial*. The paper continued:

> *The development of all of the vast regions to the north and east of Bangor has been rapid during the past 15 or 20 years. The erection of mammoth pulp mills* [in Millinocket and elsewhere] *which have caused scores of lumbering crews to be sent into the woods every season, the development of the potato growing industry and of agriculture generally in Aroostook County and the opening of new country by the construction of the Bangor & Aroostook, the Washington County, the Penobscot Central, the Somerset*

and other lines of railway have all contributed toward making the wholesale interests of Bangor one of the mainstays of business here.

Bangor no longer claimed to be the "lumber capital of the world." As the trading center of eastern and northern Maine, however, at the dawn of the state's paper and potato boom, it was doing just fine. A log didn't have to pass through the Queen City to generate money for its capitalists—its grocers, clothiers and equipment dealers and even its saloonkeepers. Thanks to the new pulp and paper mills, the lumber camps were thriving still, and they bought most of their goods from Bangor.

Bangor was the wholesale center for approximately 300,000 people, and competition from the westward was comparatively negligible. The Bangor Chapter of United Commercial Travelers (traveling salesmen) boasted 300 members, "a proportion to Bangor's population that is greater than any city in New England, except Burlington, VT," said the newspaper. Things could only get better. The open spaces north and east of the city would fill up with farmers, and waterpower possibilities would be exploited, surmised a "leading local wholesaler" interviewed by the writer.

Indeed, Bangor's population did increase by half between 1910 and 1960. But the notion that the remote rural areas to the north and east would continue swelling economically, fueling continued growth in the Queen City, faded away as the century progressed.

The largest segment of this wholesale empire was the grocery business. "It is safe to say that Bangor wholesalers in groceries have quadrupled their business during the past 25 years and it is steadily growing," said the newspaper. The largest of the wholesale grocers were Thurston & Kingsbury, T.R. Savage & Co., John Cassidy Co., Charles Hayward Co. and Arthur Chapin Co. Train carloads of goods were delivered by Bangor merchants into the hinterlands, both to the small towns and to the lumber camps deep in the woods.

Bangor was also an important jobbing center for dry goods, boots and shoes, drugs, hardware, steel and iron, cement, grain, coal, stoves, country produce, lumber, hay, salt and fish. Some of these items, like work shoes, moccasins and iron stoves, were manufactured in Bangor. Other items were shipped from distant places, never passing through the city at all. The leading wholesale houses for such products included the Adams Dry Goods Co., J.M. Arnold Shoe Co., Sawyer Boot & Shoe Co., Caldwell Sweet Co., Rice & Miller Co., Haynes & Chalmers Co., W.P. Dickey & Co., Morse & Co. and N.H. Bragg & Sons.

J.F. Parkhurst & Son Co. manufactured luggage and harnesses and sold its products in far-off places. But Frederic H. Parkhurst, the manager of one of the city's biggest employers, sought to dispel the myth that manufacturing alone was the secret to a city's success. "It is not the city of great manufacturing industries that is the largest and most prosperous, but the city that markets the products of the manufacturing centers and supplies the raw materials to them," he said. "New York is not a manufacturing center as is Lynn [Massachusetts]." Yet New York was "the gateway of commerce for the country, and takes toll coming and going…large manufacturers wherever situated must yield tribute."

In its own small way, Bangor had an opportunity to occupy that same position within its territory, according to Parkhurst, who was elected governor in 1920 but died after a short time in office.

Chapter 5

WHEN BANGOR LAUGHED

THE GREAT PORCUPINE WAR

October 25, 2004

One of the biggest fiascoes in the annals of Maine wildlife management occurred a century ago after state representative Fred I. Campbell, R-Cherryfield, decided that too many trees were being destroyed by porcupines in Washington County. The result was the Great Porcupine Slaughter of 1903–04, which eliminated eighty thousand Maine and Canadian porcupines and cost unwary taxpayers thousands of dollars.

Campbell's bill, prompted by a petition from eastern lumbermen, provided hunters with a twenty-five-cent bounty if they produced the nose and the feet of a porcupine to town treasurers. The towns were supposed to get the state to reimburse the money. Assuming about two thousand porcupines would be apprehended, lawmakers appropriated $500 for the towns for 1903.

The newspapers got word that the plan had turned into a bottomless pit shortly after state officials started counting up the returns after November 30, 1903, when the porcupine season closed. "Nine days of December make it plain that more porcupines have been killed than any newspaper correspondent dreamed of in his wildest prophecy," said the *Bangor Daily News* on December 11. "One official in the treasury department ventures the prediction that when the returns are all in, they will show about 30,000 to 40,000 porcupines killed."

The newspaper wags had a field day. "The porcupines can stand it if the state treasury can," joked one headline. Editors started referring to the program as "the porcupine war" and the state office where the returns were sent as "the porcupine bureau."

Soon, clerk Wiswell of the porcupine bureau was estimating that perhaps as many as 100,000 of the prickly beasts had died. The war would resume the next year, and nothing could be done to stop it because the legislature would not meet again until 1905. Wiswell was the kind of talkative bureaucrat reporters love to interview. He continued, "Nobody really expects to see a decrease in the number of porcupines. A bounty law was never known to accomplish that. On the contrary, I shouldn't be surprised if the people down east took to breeding porcupines for the sake of the bounty."

By February, the papers were crying fraud. Were all these porcupines real? Were they Maine porcupines or porcupines from away?

Citing the arrest of some Indians in Portland for fabricating seal noses so they could collect the one-dollar bounty currently on those animals, the *Bangor Daily News* ranted that the "wily red men" were probably manufacturing porcupine parts as well. The writer had to admit, however, that it would be difficult to create credible porcupine feet. The paper also claimed that porcupines were being killed in Canada and brought into Maine. "Nobody knows to how great an extent this has been carried on, but there is little doubt that the treasurers in the bounty towns have unknowingly paid for many hundreds of porcupines killed in New Brunswick," the reporter wrote.

Meanwhile, several small towns were chagrined to find they had to borrow money to make the bounty payments. B.L. Smith, treasurer of Marion, complained in the *Eastport Sentinel* that his town had to "hire" cash at 5 percent.

The final impact of the porcupine bounty in 1903 was not published until late in 1904 after the porcupine bureau finished counting. The grand tally was 79,752 porcupines dead for a bill of $19,938, according to the *Industrial Journal*. That was a lot of money back then. In fact, it was the same amount the state spent on the Maine Insane Hospital, triple the Maine State Prison expenditure and four times the amount spent to educate the students in the Unorganized Territory. It was ten times more than the governor's salary.

In all, 289 towns made claims, the largest coming from Eastern Maine. The winner was the little town of Wesley in Washington County, where 2,693 animals were killed for a payout of $673.25, more than the entire state appropriation. Ellsworth was second with $566.00 and Princeton third with $561.00 in claims.

Newspapers continued to squeeze a few laughs out of the story. "Porcupine Bill Is a Buster: 79,752 of the Critters Assassinated in 1903 and Still the Woods Are Full," declared the *Bangor Daily News*.

An editorial suggested that trying to eliminate the porcupine menace this way was like "trying to bail the Atlantic Ocean dry with a teaspoon." Had Representative Fred I. Campbell been trying to perpetuate a practical joke on the people of Maine, he couldn't have done a better job.

Then on November 19, the paper removed even this shred of redeeming social value, citing a state report blaming many of the state's destructive forest fires that year on hunters trying to smoke porcupines out of hollow trees and clefts in ledges.

Campbell, a lawyer, tried to defend his law in January 1905 before the legislature met. A *Bangor Daily News* story reported:

> *Men who don't know what it is to be kept awake of nights by the howling and growling and munching and crunching of the hedgehog legions may oppose; men who don't own any forests of hemlock to be eaten up like plates of ice cream may scoff, but the farmers and lumbermen, says Mr. Campbell, know that the hedgehogs are worse than dynamite.*

To update this little morality tale, I called the State Law Library and the Department of Inland Fisheries and Wildlife (DIFW). Lynn Randall at the library did some research, concluding that, yes indeed, the porcupine bounty law was repealed in 1905, just as the *Bangor Daily News* predicted. Nevertheless, the state had to pay intrepid porcupine killers an additional $17,027.00 for 1904 and $1,973.25 for a portion of 1905.

Inexplicably, the law was resurrected in 1927 and repealed again in 1939. Lawmakers got the same bright idea again in 1955, this time offering a bounty of fifty cents, and repealed it in 1967.

"Bounties have fallen out of favor in the profession of wildlife management," Mark Stadler, a biologist with DIFW, told me. That's because they usually don't work and invite fraud. Porcupines are still considered a problem by some people, especially those in forest management, he said, but their regulation has been left to Mother Nature. Good old Mother Nature.

APRIL FOOLS

March 31, 2008

Elaborate April Fools' Day jokes were once a national pastime. A century ago, the boys at the *Bangor Daily News*, in cahoots with Fire Chief William Mason, cooked up one that still provides a chuckle.

The announcement in the newspaper that April 1 morning a century ago seems a bit prosaic today. Joseph Drummond, ex-chief of the Passaic (New Jersey) Fire Department, now representing the Sims Arlington Company of Seneca Falls, New York, was in town to demonstrate one of his company's aerial firetrucks. The city was considering buying one, the story reported. Just the other day, Chief Mason had stated that it would be difficult to fight a fire in one of the growing number of tall buildings downtown with the present apparatus.

The machine was alleged to be "a splendid example of the latest thing in aerial trucks and has been much admired by those who have seen it," commented the newspaper. "The mechanism is really a sort of telescope of ladders, operated by hydraulic power, which reaches instantly almost a height of 106 feet carrying a line of hose and firemen with them."

The exhibition would be given at 11:00 a.m. at City Hall, which had a tall bell tower. "Mr. Drummond declares he can land a man with a line of hose on the bell deck of the tower in 40 seconds," reported the newspaper. Then one of Mr. Drummond's assistants, a former fireman, was going to slide from the top of the extended ladders to the ground "by means of the hand rails only."

This was back in the days when City Hall sat on the slope at the corner of Hammond and Columbia Streets. Mr. Drummond wanted to set his truck on this hill to demonstrate that it worked smoothly under any conditions. The Sims-Arlington machine had a base of only ten feet by six feet. "It is remarkable how ladders can be worked so perfectly from so small a platform," the newspaper reported drily.

This announcement aroused a good deal more interest in 1908 than it would today. This was the age of startling inventions. The telephone, the automobile, the electric light bulb, the airplane, the phonograph, the wireless and many other amazing innovations had been invented or made widely available to the public only recently. Why not a ladder that shot into space like Jack's beanstalk?

The fear of catastrophic fire frightened people then in the same way the possibility of a major terrorist attack does today. Fire equipment was

Bangor's old City Hall, with its tall bell tower, was a landmark for miles around. *Courtesy of Richard R. Shaw.*

still towed about the city by horses. Bangor wouldn't have any motorized fire equipment for several more years—not until well after the big fire of 1911. Thus, people read the newspaper story about a magical-sounding ladder on that April first morning—one powered by "hydraulics"—with considerable interest.

By 11:00 a.m., between three hundred and five hundred people, by the newspaper's estimate, had gathered at City Hall to see Chief Drummond and his wonderful contraption. They blocked the sidewalk and craned their necks in an attitude suggestive of "a large astronomy class." "They waited and waited and waited some more. Pretty soon, Chief Mason hove in sight, smiling, and the crowd could almost begin to hear the creaking of the ladders," reported the newspaper the next day. But nothing happened.

Soon, anyone with a ladder began to attract attention. A window washer working across the street for the Window and Sign Cleaning Company folded up his ladder and began to leave. The crowd began to follow him until he became upset and started to "curse in earnest Yiddish. This drove the crowd back."

At 11:15, "at last a great light began to dawn—and the way that crowd evaporated when the light really did come—the old simile of dew under a hot sun is faint in expressing it. It was magical the way they got away. At last not one single man could be found who would admit that he attended the festivities. Not one," wrote the reporter with the exuberance of one who has pulled a fast one.

Especially interested were the politicians who arrived on the scene. "One indignant alderman thought that somebody was trying to sell the city a gold brick...he went away chastened and subdued," said the paper. "The professional politicians were all worried and excited, for, at first jump, they thought somebody was getting a few 'pickings' on the quiet and that Chief Drummond, with his beanstalk, was the wheel. But there weren't any money bags in sight anywhere."

So ended one of Bangor's many April Fools' jokes run in newspapers over the years. This one performed a public service, reminding Bangoreans they would need the most modern fire equipment if they ever had a big fire downtown. The old City Hall building with the tall bell tower emerged from the fire of 1911 unscathed only to be torn down decades later for a parking lot as part of Urban Renewal.

Bangor High Boys Ran Riot

May 26, 2008

"HIGH SCHOOL BOYS HAD WILD NIGHT," declared the headline in the *Bangor Daily News* on the morning of May 15, 1908. "Threw Students Into Watering Troughs, Paraded Streets, Besieged Windsor Hotel...Police Were Kept on the Jump."

All except "Handsome Dan" Kennedy, our hero. But first, some background.

Bangoreans were used to riots of all shapes and sizes. Usually these events involved a few drunken sailors and loggers or a crowd protesting a liquor raid. Occasionally, a small army of noisy University of Maine boys marched through town on their way to the theater.

Usually, half a dozen or so big cops with nightsticks took care of things. But the ragtag mob of high school boys, reported at two hundred strong, that charged about the streets of downtown Bangor for three hours one spring night a century ago was as unusual as it was humorous to everyone but its victims—and the school board.

Bangor High School was located across the street from where the city's public library sits today. *Courtesy of Richard R. Shaw.*

While the newspaper reports never explained exactly what touched it off, the riotous behavior apparently had to do with hazing freshmen by members of the school's military cadet program. The rioters were upperclassmen. They must have been accompanied by a few friends, because there were only sixty cadets regularly enrolled, according to Principal Henry White's report that year. Their targets were a handful of freshmen, who ran through the streets of downtown Bangor like scared rabbits chased by a pack of dogs.

Events began early in the evening after the school's battalion of military cadets was dismissed from drill in the high school yard on Harlow Street (where the Abbott Square parking lot is located today, across from the Bangor Public Library). They were supposed to be preparing for a military ball to be held later that month. But something else was in the air. Hardly had they finished when members seized one of their number and drenched him under the pump that supplied the school's drinking water.

A procession then formed for a march up the street to the watering trough in East Market Square (where City Hall is today). Another freshman was produced and ceremonially dunked. From there, the students swept across the Kenduskeag Bridge and on into Haymarket Square (where the KeyBank complex is today, across from Pickering Square). A third freshman was thrown into the local watering trough. "This time the victim was about half drowned, only the tip of his nose showing above the sluggish water," wrote the *Bangor Daily News* reporter.

The crowd of onlookers was growing, and the police were becoming quite interested. "Patrolmen Meade and Reagan came up from the [Devil's Half] acre and interfered," the newspaper reported.

Instead of breaking up the festivities, however, the boys retreated up the street to the Unitarian Church at Union and Main, where they met up with yet another opponent—a popular police officer described in the *Daily News* as "Handsome Dan Kennedy, Beau Brummel of the police force and custodian between 6:30 and midnight of the destinies of upper Main Street."

Kennedy was a favorite of the boys. "He knows how to handle 'em— remembers that he was a boy once himself, and so they listened respectfully to his suggestion that they go elsewhere," recounted the newspaper. They headed back downtown to the Nickel movie theater on Central Street, where another freshman was hiding inside. "They wanted to go in, but Manager Forrest had opposite views and the sight of four patrolmen and a half dozen unsentimental ushers drawn up across the entrance to the big lobby had a quieting effect," reported the newspaper.

Meanwhile, the freshman, who was apparently a bit sharper than his fellows, slipped out a side door and, eluding his pursuers, ran up the street into the nearby Windsor Hotel at the corner of Harlow and Franklin Streets.

The Windsor Hotel before it burned in the fire of 1911. *Courtesy of Richard R. Shaw.*

Discovering how they had been outwitted, the student mob surrounded the big hotel. A huge crowd assembled to watch the antics. Hotel staff blocked the doors. Students ran up fire escapes expecting to find their prey in one of the rooms. "For a little while, affairs assumed the proportions of almost a real riot," commented the reporter hopefully.

Half an hour later, the boys realized they had been outwitted again. With the help of hotel staff and a police officer, the intended victim had been dressed up in the head chef's white apron and coat. With the collar pulled up high, he had walked out the door, pushed through the crowd and disappeared into the evening.

After this disappointment, one more victim was given a choice between making a speech and getting a dunking in nearby Center Park. He chose the dunking.

Then the partying was about over, and the reporter for the *Bangor Daily News* retreated to his headquarters on Exchange Street to rattle out a story that would give readers a smile the next morning.

Principal Henry White and the school board, however, were not amused. Several boys were suspended for a brief period until they could be brought before the board. Punishment was then deferred until the committee found out "whether they or others contemplate any repetition of the outrage."

About this same time, a large group of grammar school students at the Union Square School decided to put on their own display of "class spirit." Once again, Patrolman Kennedy came to the rescue. They were quickly dissuaded by "Handsome Dan," or "Diplomatic Dan," as he was also known in the pages of the *Bangor Daily News*.

ESCAPE OF EUGENE, THE MAYOR'S PIG

October 18, 2010

Back in the days before supermarkets, many Bangoreans kept farm animals, ranging from cows to chickens, and planted large gardens in their yards. They were not supposed to let their animals roam around the streets, however, and when Mayor John Woodman's seven-month-old pig, Eugene, escaped from his sty at the mayor's Pine Street home a century ago, it caused a great commotion.

"Nothing which has happened here since the election, and very little before, has caused so much excitement," exclaimed a gleeful reporter for the

The view down Exchange Street to Union Station. Note the Bijou Theater sign on the right. *Courtesy of Richard R. Shaw.*

Bangor Daily Commercial on September 28, 1910. What a fine opportunity for a reporter for a Democratic newspaper to embarrass a Republican mayor! If the mayor couldn't even keep his pig under control, what could he do?

"MAYOR'S PIG OUT," declared the overwrought headline. "Great Excitement in Wild Chase Down Exchange Street." It was rumored that the mayor liked roast pork and applesauce, so naturally everyone wanted to help him catch Eugene.

After forcing his way through some loose boards in his pen, the wily Eugene started trotting downtown. Almost at once, a number of the small boys who invariably were hanging about on street corners back then spotted the escapee and gave chase.

Eugene was a pig of uncommon ingenuity, although it seems he may have underestimated his pursuers. "The pig regarded them gravely until they were within a few yards of him," the newspaper reported. "He then gave a flip of his small ringed tail and a grunt of derision after which he turned and galloped off in the direction of State Street with the boys in pursuit."

These boys were doing their civic duty by helping out the busy mayor. "He's Mayor Woodman's pig, and we're trying to catch him," they shouted breathlessly to every passerby.

"The cavalcade of pursuers grew amazingly, and by the time the bewildered pig turned onto Exchange Street, nearly half a hundred men and boys were in full chase," the newspaper reported. "His squeals could be heard nearly to City Hall."

Others tried to stop Eugene but failed. "In front of the Sterns building, Bobbie, a Scotch collie belonging to Frank C. Hinckley, started to head the pig back toward the foot of State Street. But defining the dog's purpose, Eugene feigned a tack to starboard, came about suddenly to port and passed on unhindered."

The wild chase continued toward the busy train station at the end of the street, proving Eugene was no slouch in city traffic. "Threading his way in and out, through carriages and teams and past trolley cars and astonished pedestrians on the crosswalks, Eugene continued his mad career down Exchange Street, followed by the excited, yelling crowd of men and boys which was increasing in numbers."

But his moments of freedom were numbered. Eugene was becoming winded. Union Station blocked his way at the foot of Exchange Street. The crowd was closing in.

In an effort to evade the shouting, laughing mob, Eugene headed onto the walkway that led from the street to the drawbridge across the Kenduskeag Stream. Meanwhile, a particularly skilled group of railroad employees including Guy Hewey, foreman of car inspection, and car inspectors Cavanaugh and Whitney had joined the chase, motivated by a desire to protect railroad property and keep anyone from getting hurt.

After a number of successful dodges, weary Eugene was cornered by Inspector Whitney. "As the railroad men fell upon him, Eugene gave vent to a series of squeals which could be heard all over that part of the city. Eugene was securely anchored in a coal pocket until Mayor Woodman, who was notified of his escape and recapture, could send a man to take him home," the story concluded.

The mayor's reaction went unrecorded—not even whether he promised Eugene's captors a pork chop or two.

WHEN THE REVEREND BERRY DID THE HOOCHEE-COOCHEE

January 10, 2011

Surely, the day the Reverend Mr. Wilbur F. Berry, superintendent of the Christian Civic League of Maine, performed the "Hoochie-Coochee" at one

Located near Union Station, the Penobscot Exchange was one of the city's finer hotels. *Courtesy of Richard R. Shaw.*

of Bangor's finest hotels before a convocation of dignitaries deserves at least a footnote in local history books. The League, an influential player in Maine politics then and now, frequently made its presence known in the Queen City, visiting saloons and gambling dens in an effort to get public officials to enforce vice laws. The group's target this time was the Eastern Maine State Fair, where there had been longstanding rumors of immorality on the midway.

The state's commissioner of agriculture, A.W. Gilman, and the assistant attorney general, Charles P. Barnes, came to Bangor on December 20, 1910, to listen to Berry's charges at a hearing in the clubroom at the Penobscot Exchange, the big hotel located just up Exchange Street from Union Station. At stake was the stipend given to the agricultural fairs each year by the state to promote farming. If Berry could prove fair managers had allowed an immoral act to appear, Commissioner Gilman would have to withhold the cash, which amounted to $1,750 (nearly $40,000 in today's money), according to the *Bangor Daily Commercial*. Fair officials had already spent that amount last summer.

Mr. Berry was the only witness. He said that on August 25 he had visited one of the midway acts staged by vaudeville impresario "Diamond Lew"

Walker. Berry paid the ten-cent admission to see this particular show twice that day, both in the morning and in the afternoon. The show was divided into two parts. The Reverend Berry objected to part of the first part, in which a young woman performed a "Spanish dance." Her clothing was modest enough, said the minister, but her movements were immoral.

After the act ended, the barker had promised an even steamier show if the gentlemen in the audience would pay an additional twenty-five cents and step into a nearby "annex." There, they "might see the dance as it was danced when John the Baptist lost his head," giving the act biblical overtones.

Many of the men, including Mr. Berry, paid their quarters, but the result was a letdown. Inside the annex, a girl "in a cabinet" wearing pink tights and "a flounce about her hips" did some "poses," which were so unobjectionable that Superintendent Berry did not include them in his complaint.

Then, adding insult to injury, the original young woman of the infamous Spanish dance reappeared and rudely dismissed the crowd, saying, "You bald-headed sinners are as bad in Bangor as anywhere else. You're the easiest group of suckers that ever bit a bare hook."

Commissioner Gilman said he was puzzled about the Reverend Berry's notion of immorality. He asked him to re-enact the Spanish dance. "Could you put your body in the same positions?" he asked (perhaps with a little smile quivering around the corners of his mouth?).

"I shouldn't care to," responded the witness modestly.

"Then how am I to know that the dance was immoral?"

Mr. Berry replied that if the stenographer (apparently a female) was sent out of the room, he would attempt to show those assembled what he meant. After all the testimony had been taken and the stenographer had left, he then agreed to put on a little demonstration. He went through various "grotesque motions," reported the *Commercial*, barely suppressing its editorial laughter.

During this ridiculous display, Flavius O. Beal, one of the fair owners and a former Bangor mayor, said he didn't see anything immoral about it. "It looks to me just like the motions a lame man would make in turning around, and I haven't heard of any lame men being held up because they acted immorally."

The *Commercial*, which had a longstanding feud with the League, exhibited its story jubilantly that evening with this sensational headline: "REV. MR. BERRY DOES THE 'HOOCHEE-COOCHEE' DANCE.'"

Berry was questioned closely about why he had waited weeks to file his complaint instead of doing it the day of his investigation. He replied that two years ago, a detective employed by the League had been rudely rebuffed by local officials when he reported gambling at the fair. Berry also said that the part of the act that he objected to was dropped at his behest at later fairs in several Maine towns and cities, hinting other communities might be just a little more moral than the Queen City, a thought highly offensive to Bangor's leaders.

Berry said he had never seen such a dance "in the lowest theater that I have visited." He was asked to define an immoral show. The statute defined it as "any show that tends to corrupt the morals of youth." Berry added, "If you had seen the looks on the faces in that tent and seen the nudges between the men, you would have believed it immoral alright."

Speaking in defense of the fair were fourteen witnesses including the mayor, fair officials, several policemen and the police chief and Levi B. Walker, "Diamond Lew" himself. They all agreed the dance display had been properly modest and the fair had been the cleanest in history. "I guarantee a good show for the price," said Lew nonchalantly, adding he believed the Spanish dancer was proper for anyone to see.

A few weeks later, Commissioner Gilman issued his predictable decision. "THE WIGGLE DANCE WASN'T IMMORAL," crowed the *Bangor Daily News* on January 3, 1911. While that newspaper favored prohibition, it had little use for the Civic League's tactics. The complaint was dismissed. The fair association got its money. If anything objectionable was introduced into the program, it must have been done secretly against the instructions of officials, said Commissioner Gilman.

The fair would doubtless continue to be on its guard next year, however, as were the Queen City's saloonkeepers and slot machine proprietors. You could never tell when Civic League spies might be in the crowd.

BULL VS. AUTO

September 19, 2011

This headline appeared in the *Bangor Daily Commercial* on June 29, 1911: "BULL CHARGES AUTO: Two Women Saved by O'Connor's Revolver on Ellsworth Road."

The heroic age of the automobile occurred about a century ago. Besides mechanical aptitude, you needed a lot of courage to drive one of the new machines. Stories about the difficult conditions that flourished were legion. Hazards included potholes the size of small ponds and frequent mechanical breakdowns and flat tires. Angry farm animals were also a risk, as the above headline indicates. Usually, these animal stories involved runaway horses, sometimes with tragic consequences. At least once, however, an angry bull locked horns with a hapless autoist near the Queen City of the East.

Hermann Stott, a New York mining engineer, was traveling on the Ellsworth Road toward Bangor when his bright red automobile stalled next to a pasture owned by farmer Sumner Smith. In the words of the reporter, who probably did not own an automobile, "something happened to the magneto," interrupting the journey and causing everyone to pile out of the machine. The passengers included Mrs. Stott; Miss Bertha Taylor of Bloomfield, New Jersey; and George O'Connor of New York.

While Stott and O'Connor looked under the hood, the two ladies stood a little too close to the nearby farm fence. Roads were a lot narrower than they are today, so they probably didn't have much choice. Presiding over the pasture was a large Jersey bull, who, it was believed, took umbrage at the flaming color of the Stotts' auto. Before anybody noticed, the bull had broken through the fence "almost without warning." Then the carnage began.

The bull made quick work of the auto. "There were shrieks and a fluttering of white skirts as the animal came up against the side of the automobile with a force which nearly turned it over," reported the newspaper. "For a moment or two, the bull stood dazed by the impact. Then, with a bellow of rage, he charged straight at the two women, who had started on the run for a stone wall a few yards distant."

It is unclear where the men were hiding, but there appeared little chance of escape for the ladies, and Mr. Stott closed his eyes to shut out the sight. Then he fainted.

O'Connor, meanwhile, had been rummaging around in "the bottom of the tonneau" (the rear seating compartment) for his traveling bag, which contained his automatic revolver. "He at length succeeded in getting the bag open and gaining possession of the weapon. As he raised it and fired, Mrs. Stott sprained her ankle and went down, the bull passing directly over her and crashing to the ground with a bullet through his heart," reported the newspaper.

Meanwhile, Miss Taylor had made it to the stone wall but was "badly bruised about the face in falling over the other side."

Before leaving the scene of this disaster, Mr. Stott regained consciousness soon enough to reach "a satisfactory settlement" with Farmer Smith, whose bull had smashed a running board and mudguard of the flaming red automobile.

Then the group re-boarded and chugged away to Bangor, apparently little the worse for wear except for the two ladies, who were treated by a local physician. The fate of the magneto, for those who know what this device was, went unrecorded.

It is interesting to note that the newspaper scribe recorded the make of the bull but not the make of the auto, an unusual lapse back in those days when people were familiar with horse and cattle breeds but much more interested in auto brands.

There are plenty of other adventure stories about autos in the Bangor papers from this period. Nearly 8,500 of these machines were registered in Maine by the summer of 1911. Speed demons were setting records. Accidents were becoming more common. Automobilists were appearing increasingly at places like the Eastern Maine State Fair in Bangor, Riverside Park in Hampden and at major resort hotels, presaging a whole new era in recreation. There was even a new type of bandit, who motored to banks, robbed them and then drove off in a cloud of dust. But I have seen only one story about a bull attacking an auto.

Chapter 6

THE LIQUOR WAR

LIQUOR WAR ON AGAIN IN BANGOR

December 29, 2003

"Liquor War is On Again in Bangor," shouted a bold, black headline in the *Bangor Daily News* three days before Christmas 1903. "Seventeen Warrants Out and Seven Seizures Made Last Night—County Attorney After the Uno Men."

The cozy relationship between saloonkeepers and the law was being disrupted once again.

"Things have been going so quietly of late that many of the liquor dealers of Bangor and a good many other people, too, had come to the conclusion that the cruel war inaugurated last June was over," led the reporter.

County Attorney Bertram Smith obtained arrest warrants Monday afternoon, and by 7:00 p.m., a small army of deputy sheriffs and city cops had raided seventeen saloons—or tried to.

Someone had tipped off most of the miscreants, and ten of the shops were closed. Activity was found in only seven establishments run mostly by men with such ethnic names as Moriarty, Doherty, McCurdy and Boudreau. They were conducting business at dives on Harlow, Exchange and Broad Streets and even at the famed Bangor House, the city's best hotel.

Several pitchers were smashed as the bartenders tried to dump the goods, and Deputy Emerson cut his hand in one such "mix up." Some of the barmen said they were only selling "good old uno beer," which had a very low alcohol content, so samples had to be sent for analysis in a couple of cases.

Smith and Sheriff Lindley Gilman were only getting warmed up. On Tuesday morning, they herded the culprits through court. Federal tax records showing the names of liquor dealers who had paid the U.S. government a federal fee to get their booze were used to convict some of them whether or not any liquor was actually found on the premises. That evening, Smith and Gilman headed for Old Town with a posse to conduct more raids.

"But every place visited was as bare as Mother Hubbard's famous cupboard," commented the NEWS correspondent, who found the activity quite humorous. "The proprietors did not appear to be overwhelmed by surprise and greeted the visitors with smiles."

The next Monday, however, the raiders launched a surprise attack, rounding up six saloonkeepers on Lower Water Street, at the City Hotel and Cousins Hotel and at Basin Mills at a watering hole known as Joe Pooler's Place. Once again, things went peacefully, except Mr. Cousins, the hotel proprietor, took flight and remained missing several days later.

The next day, the liquor business in Old Town "was rather demoralized," and lookouts had been posted at the doors of the places that were still open, noted the correspondent, who seemed to know where all the saloons were along with everyone else in town.

A few days later, this traveling vaudeville show moved across the river to Brewer, where "the largest seizure of liquor" in the city's history was made. A "sled load" of booze was found stored in the cellar of a house at King's Court allegedly intended for use in the adjoining South Brewer Hotel. The bartender was arrested for selling liquor to a young boy, a possible reference to a newspaper story a few days before describing the plight of "two little newsboys" who were found staggering about "blind drunk" in Bangor.

What is one to make of all this mayhem, accompanied by tongue-in-cheek newspaper coverage as if it were all a practical joke on the public? Well, of course, it was to the weary reporters, who knew the liquor dealers would all be up and running again in a few days and that many people didn't care.

For more than half a century, liquor sales had been illegal in Maine. Citizens had even enshrined prohibition in their state constitution. Yet the law was a shambles, and liquor flowed like water in Bangor and a few other cities. There was little agreement on how the law should be enforced or whether it should be enforced at all.

Republicans tended to be pro-prohibition, while Democrats wanted to get rid of what had come to be nationally known as the "Maine Law" because

Maine was the first state to go dry. Federal Prohibition was still more than a decade away, and the eyes of the country were on the Pine Tree State as the movement expanded to other states.

How Maine's law was enforced all depended on what sheriff was in office or what judge was on the bench. The Reverend R.E. Smith of the Pine Street Methodist Church had delivered a stinging sermon printed in the *Bangor Daily News* that called the current conditions "a giant octopus, which has cuddled our city in its many slimy and treacherous arms."

On the other hand, Mayor Flavius O. Beal expressed to reporters his opposition to the law and the impact crackdowns had on driving liquor use out of respectable saloons into the "kitchen bars" and onto the streets, where "pocket peddlers" did a brisk business. "Why, on Saturday when I went to the wharf to board the steamer to Islesboro, I saw six men drinking out of bottles in a sneaking sort of way," he complained.

Bangor was one of the most notorious watering spots in the state. It was estimated that there had been 150 saloons at the beginning of 1903, but this number had dropped to 30 or 40 by July for at least a few weeks because of stepped-up enforcement.

Arrests for public drunkenness had soared from 895 to 1,236 in four years, surpassing all other crimes many times over—a sure sign there was plenty of liquor to be had. The city's name was even attached to a system—the Bangor Plan—used to nullify the law completely in Bangor and some other towns. Maine journalist Holman Day described how it worked in a magazine story in 1908:

> *The sheriff and county attorney allowed a certain number of saloons and hotels to sell liquor. Prior to the term of court at which fines were to be "assessed," the county attorney, or his agent, went to the office of the collector of internal revenue at Portsmouth, NH and drew off a list of names of those in the county who were paying a special liquor retailer's tax to the United States government. Then the county attorney presented the list to the grand jury, and it was accepted as evidence that each party was a dealer in liquor. The parties were accordingly indicted on that evidence alone and accepted the indictment without protest and came up to the "cap'n's" office and settled without demur. Each paid the regular fine and costs amounting to one hundred and ten dollars. Usually the county "assessed" twice a year.*

The Bangor Plan paid the county's debts and built a new courthouse, said Day.

Higher fines and threats of jail time recently had clearly shaken up the cozy system that had evolved between Bangor and its saloonkeepers. The Reverend Smith and his parishioners and others like them were fed up with the hypocrisy.

The drama that was going on at Christmastime 1903 was only a short chapter in a long-running soap opera that would not end for another thirty-one years, when Mainers finally overturned their constitutional amendment banning liquor sales. It was nearly a year after national Prohibition was repealed.

ROTTEN BANGOR:
WHEN CARRY NATION STORMED THE QUEEN CITY

June 7, 2004

Maine was a beacon for the nation before the Civil War when it became the first state to ban liquor. By the first years of the twentieth century, however, the Maine law was a joke to many, and with its dozens of barrooms, Bangor was one of the most infamous places to buy a drink. Even the notorious saloon smasher Carry Nation couldn't put things to right when she roared into the Queen City toting her hatchet and Bible in late August 1902.

Nation got off on the wrong foot from the start. She never forgave Bangor for the indignities heaped upon her. On the way to the Bangor House, where she had a room reserved, she asked the carriage driver where the "dives" were in town. He obligingly gave her a list that included the famous hotel where she was staying. In fact, it happened to be the very hotel where President Theodore Roosevelt, the man Nation called a "beer-slinging Dutchman," had spoken on a campaign swing only a couple of days before.

There are two versions of what happened after Nation got to the hotel, one printed in local papers and the other in Nation's autobiography.

According to the locals, who, it can be argued, were all in cahoots, Nation sat down in the dining room and asked for beer. "When informed that she could not have any beer, she repeated her demand in a loud voice and soon was the centre of all eyes. The hotel people say she created a scene, such as they are not used to at the Bangor House," according to the account in the *Bangor Semi-Weekly News* on September 2, 1902.

"Capt. H.C. Chapman, the senior proprietor of the hotel came into the dining room and asked Mrs. Nation to leave, and when she indignantly

Carry Nation tried to buy a glass of beer at the Bangor House, the city's finest hotel, with disastrous consequences. *Courtesy of Richard R. Shaw.*

refused, he led her from the room and, accompanied by one of the clerks, to her own apartments, where her things were packed up. Then Capt. Chapman escorted the smasher to the Union St. entrance and put her out upon the sidewalk, where Deputy Chief of Police Bowen and Patrolman Sproul, who had been sent for when the crowd began to gather, took her in charge, bundled her into a carriage and drove to the City Hall [where she was to deliver a lecture that night]," said the newspaper report.

Nation's account differs substantially. After she was promised a bottle of beer by a waitress, Chapman appeared. Nation wrote:

> *He rushed up to me in a drunken rage. He threw me against one of the pillars, then literally knocked me out into the hall in the presence of the guests, perhaps a hundred; then he kept knocking me down every time I rose to my feet. He would not allow me to get my things. This Chapman was a noted dive keeper, a rummy, and ran a representative rum-soaked republican hotel.*

That night she railed against Chapman and the Bangor House in "a rambling talk, incoherent and disjointed," according to a local newspaper reporter. What had been intended as an account of her recent saloon-smashing spree in Kansas turned into a violent denunciation of Bangor and Republicans, who controlled the state. Afterward, she sold her photographs and her trademark little gold hatchets embossed with her name. She spent the night at the home of one Dr. Marshall, a prohibitionist, after being told there wasn't a hotel in Bangor that would put her up. Of course, all the hotels offered liquor. It was rumored she planned to tour the city the next day in search of some saloons to smash.

But the next day, Carry Nation was "frozen out" of Bangor, according to the local reporter, using the most acidic sarcasm he could muster to prove he had no sympathies with the maven of temperance. That morning, a Saturday, she was ejected from the Columbia Building after giving a judge and other officials a tongue-lashing because they refused to issue a warrant for the arrest of Captain Chapman.

After calling Deputy Bowen one of "hell's scullions," she "played hide and seek with the Penobscot Bar (legal) and had dignified attorneys crawling head first into waste baskets" as she searched unsuccessfully for counsel.

Then, to add insult to injury, she was informed by the mayor that she could not speak in City Hall again that night.

She was on the steamer *City of Rockland* by afternoon, carrying her rampage against Bangor to a Boston rostrum, where she pulled up her sleeve and showed a mass of bruises above her elbow as evidence of her assault at the Bangor House. There were more such marks on her back, she told the crowd, which "howled" when she promised not to show them. "Bangor is so rotten, I could not even get a lawyer," she told the Boston crowd.

But that would not be the last Bangor would hear from Carry Nation. She returned to Maine two years later on her way to Canada. This time she was more circumspect in her approach, her treatment of "rotten" Bangor more subdued. With no fanfare, she arrived in Eastport on the steamer *St. Croix* on April 12, 1904. She got off the boat long enough to march down Water Street with a crowd at her heels, stopping in front of Captain Charles Dines's billiard hall. She entered, threatening "to break out a few windows and close out the joint in quick time." But she took no action, getting back on the boat and heading for St. John and later Fredericton, New Brunswick, where her lectures enjoyed receptive audiences.

Nation returned to Canada late in May, making some whistle stops in Maine. "When she struck Bangor, her ire was aroused by memories of her previous visit," wrote a reporter for the *Bangor Daily News*. She got off the train long enough to bawl out a man for smoking a pipe and a couple of youngsters puffing on cigarettes. "They sassed her," the press reported.

After another successful visit to Canada, she returned to Bangor at the end of June—a century ago this month—where she was allowed back into City Hall to lecture to a small but appreciative audience.

The next day, realizing that much of her thunder had been stolen by the state's Republican nominating convention, Nation gave two more speeches nearer the Bangor Auditorium, where the event was taking place. In the morning she delivered a "tirade" in which she "cussed the Republican Party up hill and down and back again" to a group of about five hundred waiting in line to get into the convention. That afternoon she gave another talk to a less sympathetic group, the members of which "were inclined to give the crusader the laff" from the steps of a nearby grocery store.

Of course, all of these events were followed by the sale of her "little pearl hatchets with glass diamonds in them," prompting a cynical Bangor press scribe to ask, "Which is closer to Carry's heart: the temperance problem, or the profits on the little hatchets?"

It is easy to lose sight of Carry Nation's significance in all this jocularity, but despite her eccentricities she was a major figure in both the temperance and women's movements. Her popularity, even among those who drank and smoked, only underscored the fact that the Maine Law didn't work. In a few years, the federal government would move in and try to do a better job.

Judge Chapman's Impeachment

March 26, 2007

Maine's battle against booze registered a new milestone of melodramatic ferocity early in March 1907 when Judge Harry J. Chapman of the Bangor Municipal Court was impeached by the legislature. The Reverend Henry N. Pringle, field secretary of the Christian Civic League of Maine, had been snooping around Bangor for months collecting evidence that the judge was not enforcing the state prohibition law. Now he was using his influence in an attempt to get the judge rolled out of the Queen City in a whiskey barrel.

Pringle was a "liquor spotter," one of the class of vigilantes who spent their days trying to get the legal establishment to enforce the Maine Law. But during the Chapman fiasco, the *Bangor Daily News* questioned his abilities as a detective. "For a man who has…battled with the devil, he has a surprisingly unsophisticated demeanor," the newspaper commented. At certain moments, he "looked as though one could have sold him a gold brick at 100 cents on the dollar."

A temperance ally, Representative Marcellus J. Dow of Brooks introduced a resolve in the legislature calling for Chapman's impeachment on eight charges. The judge stood accused of "nullifying" the law by failing to convict liquor dealers or by not sentencing them to jail terms. The most sensational allegation was that Chapman had favored liquor men who stocked their barrooms with cigars sold by the Madine Cigar Company, of which he was president and a stockholder.

The judge was also charged with coddling the *Bangor Daily Commercial*, which ran liquor advertisements in violation of state law. Pringle had pressured several other newspapers to stop running the ads, but the *Commercial* asserted it had constitutional rights. The feud had become so bitter that the newspaper started spelling Pringle's name with a lowercase "p" to express its contempt for him.

Many of the cases introduced as evidence at Chapman's impeachment hearings had resulted from attempts by Pringle and his two assistants to entrap liquor dealers. At the establishment of William S. Newman at 114 Haymarket Square, for example, Pringle described "how the barkeepers were continually ordering coffee up the dumbwaiter and how whiskey always came back." Pringle ordered and tasted some of the "coffee" to make sure he had hard evidence.

This mode of operation had its risks. During the controversy that erupted over the prosecution of Newman, Pringle claimed he was taken aside by one Albert L. Blanchard, a lawyer, and told "that if I continued to disturb things around in the community he would give me the worst carding I ever got, and it would last an hour." (In April, Pringle was badly beaten in Bar Harbor by a mob after he pressed charges against a "pocket peddler" who sold him liquor.)

Such testimony filled the Chapman impeachment proceeding, which lasted from March 20 to 22. Some of the most damaging was provided by Penobscot County Attorney Hervey Patten. He had boycotted Chapman's court after the judge discharged his cases for lack of evidence even though police had seized liquor.

Nothing seemed out of order in regards to Chapman's overall performance, however, according to Frank A. Adams, clerk of the Bangor Municipal Court for fourteen years. He said that out of 234 search-and-seizure cases from January 12, 1905, to March 5, 1907, there had been jail sentences in 59 and fines and costs in 112. He said the proceedings were no different today than they had ever been.

Chapman had been judge only two years. "If this man is guilty, what's the matter with stringing up about three quarters of the police judges in Maine," remarked a disgruntled state representative from Androscoggin County.

Chapman's lawyers also produced statistics purporting to show that he didn't treat liquor dealers who were customers of the Madine Cigar Company any differently than other violators. Big purchasers of the company's products went to jail just like little ones. So what if one of the company's brands was called "The Judge's Choice"?

The proceedings produced plenty of colorful rhetoric. No one was calling for Judge Chapman's removal except Pringle, who was not even a resident of Bangor, noted one of the judge's lawyers. "I say as compared to honorable manhood, this man Pringle is like a crawling reptile," one of them ranted.

A lawyer for the temperance group countered that "things…were getting so rotten in Bangor that someone had to come to the rescue and it just happened to devolve upon Mr. Pringle to pull the good people of the city out of the mire of iniquity."

The *Bangor Daily News*' own assessment of the evidence against Chapman before any votes had been taken proved prophetic: "On certain counts there was not enough direct and irrevocable testimony to convict a fly for being wantonly, willfully and illegally around the bung-hole of a molasses barrel."

The House crushed the prosecution on March 25. Only the cigar factory accusation generated much concern, losing on a vote of fifty to forty-one. The next day, the Senate dismissed the charges "like dew before the sun," the *Bangor Daily News* rhapsodized. An actual vote was taken on only one issue, the cigar factory conflict, and it resulted in a sixteen-to-ten acquittal.

Judge Chapman had emerged from this debacle with his honor intact. But illegal barrooms still dotted the Queen City. If Judge Chapman and others were doing their jobs, why were these places still around?

Judge Chapman's Revenge

June 25, 2007

Evil could lurk in unlikely places a century ago. Your moral well-being might be at risk in a restaurant, a fruit stand or even a pawn shop.

One of the more nefarious manifestations of evil was the slot machine, which popped up like dandelions in Bangor whenever virtue turned its back.

In the spring of 1907, many of these "nickel in the slot" machines dispensed cigars to winners. Slots that paid out actual cash seemed to be keeping a very low profile at that time in the Queen City.

One of the greatest enforcers of virtue—a "spotter" in the parlance of the day—was the Reverend Henry N. Pringle, field secretary of the Christian Civic League of Maine. He appeared in the Queen City on Monday, June 24, to swear out a warrant against several proprietors of business establishments harboring slots. Then, accompanied by an intrepid band of sheriff's deputies, namely Emerson, Spratt, Powers and Friend, the Waterville minister set out to crush these dens of iniquity where a man could deposit a coin in the hopes of winning a cigar.

By the end of the trip, the men had seized nine machines—one from P.H. McNamara's store on Exchange Street; two from Paul Martini, a fruit dealer at the corner of Central and Harlow Streets; two at Charles Adams's restaurant on Hammond Street; and two more at the Rialto restaurant on Main Street, where Frank Daley was the proprietor. Perhaps the strangest catch of the day, however, was the raid at Max Cohen's pawnshop on Exchange Street, where two more of the devilish devices were expropriated.

Tuesday morning, several of the defendants and their lawyers appeared in the Bangor Municipal Court before Judge Harry J. Chapman. He ordered the machines destroyed. Only McNamara appealed.

The mere destruction of these insidious devices, however, was not enough for Pringle. He also had sworn out warrants accusing the men of running gambling establishments. The fireworks did not begin until Wednesday, when the defendants reappeared in court to face the charges.

Pringle and Chapman had a longstanding feud. Pringle had tried to have Chapman impeached by the legislature in March for not enforcing the state prohibition law. Ironically, one of the charges Pringle had leveled against the part-time judge was that he owned a cigar factory and showed favoritism to saloonkeepers who stocked his brands. Pringle had failed miserably in this endeavor. All his charges were crushed by state lawmakers. He emerged from that donnybrook looking something like a fool. Now it was time for Judge Chapman to get his revenge.

Pringle got into trouble almost immediately on Wednesday when he tried to participate in the hearing along with the lawyers and sheriff's deputies. As the case at Adams's restaurant was being heard, he rose to his feet:

"Your honor..."

"Sit down," said the judge.

"But in this place machines were removed and put back."

"That makes no difference. You sit down."

Meanwhile, Adams's lawyer, Frank Plumstead, commented that his client's offense was only a minor one. Playing a machine for cigars was no worse than buying books of chance or reaching into a grab bag at a church fair. Bringing a respectable citizen to court on gambling charges after he had consented to the destruction of the machines was a burlesque, the lawyer complained.

The Martini case elicited another clash between the Reverend Pringle and Judge Chapman.

"Your honor…" interrupted Pringle, jumping to his feet.

"Sit down."

"But your honor…"

"You sit down. I can attend to these cases myself. All you want is a conviction. Now sit down or I will fine you," shouted Judge Chapman. And that was the last heard from the Reverend Pringle in the judge's courtroom that day—at least in the pages of Bangor's two daily newspapers.

The Reverend Pringle got what he wanted, however. Adams, Daley and Martini were found guilty, and each was fined about ten dollars. Only Max Cohen emerged unscathed. Testimony revealed that the machines at his pawnshop had been left there by a man who had since died. They were being stored pending settlement of the estate. "Not guilty," said the judge.

Poor Pringle won most of his cases, but as usual, he emerged looking battered and broken in the newspapers. Abuse was heaped upon him by nearly everyone. Martini's lawyer, Donald Snow, described his client as "a man who does more work in one day than any 30 cent reformer in the state does in a month." Others accused Pringle of filing the cases and previous ones to collect witness fees from the court. The *Bangor Daily Commercial* reporter went so far as to call him "the officious official of the officious league." The *Commercial* was an anti-prohibition paper that catered to Democrats. Pringle had instigated a lawsuit to force its owners to stop running illegal liquor advertising.

It would take another century before a slot machine would be regarded by the state as a means to fatten its purse rather than as a one-armed devil. The Reverend Henry Pringle and the majority of Mainers back then would be surprised and disheartened to see how things have changed in favor of the "nickel in the slot."

STURGIS MEN INVADE

August 20, 2007

"LIKE A THUNDERBOLT THE DEPUTIES STRUCK...Pounced Upon Liquor Dealers, Tied 'Em Up and Nailed 'Em Down." So read part of the *Bangor Daily News*' lead headline on Monday morning, August 19, 1907. The long-expected Sturgis Commission blitzkrieg had finally rolled into the Queen City.

For weeks, rumors had been abroad. The much-feared Sturgis deputies were about to raid Bangor. The commission had been established in a burst of enthusiasm by the Maine Legislature to enforce the state liquor law in those towns where locals weren't doing the job. Everyone knew Bangor was enforcing the law haphazardly at best.

Saturday was S-Day for the Queen City. Sturgis men had been sniffing around town under cover. That evening, a dozen agents, divided into four squads, started draining one of the city's watering holes after another. First they had to get by "the wireless"—the system of lookouts stationed outside the bars to spot approaching lawmen.

But Sturgis men were strangers to Bangor. "They passed the lookouts without question and were as welcome as a Rory [a thirsty logger] off a 100 days drive," said the *Bangor Daily News*, borrowing a metaphor from the

Detectives working for the Sturgis Commission in Bangor stored liquor they seized in a room on Franklin Street. *Courtesy of Richard R. Shaw.*

logging industry that would have been familiar to every reader. "The liquor dealers of the city were completely outwitted."

The alarm spread quickly, however. "As it was fully known that the [log] jam was started, there was the greatest hustle for the shore known in years," according to the colorful *Bangor Daily News* writer. "The 'wireless' was red hot. Telephones jingled in scores of barrooms. Customers were hustled out, doors locked, curtains drawn, stocks dumped or rushed to hiding places." That night, "crowds gathered on the street corners…intense excitement prevailed. Thirsty pilgrims meandered through Hodgdon Street, around Pickering Square, down Broad Street and 'The Acre,' and found every gin-mill quiet and dark. Lower Exchange Street was in gloom."

The first raid occurred shortly after 6:00 p.m. at Maurice P. Gallagher's place on Central Street. It was necessary to use a wagon to carry all the booze away. And so it went for weeks, the prizes getting harder to find as even the most brazen dealers ducked underground.

One of the strangest seizures a few days into the invasion was two barrels of ale hidden under the steps of the Bangor Auditorium at the corner of Buck and Main Streets, a place normally reserved for opera performances. Clement Smith had been seen rolling one barrel from the barn at the nearby Commercial House, where he conducted a liquor business, to the auditorium steps.

The Sturgis men threatened to pull out all stops. Chief Deputy Ferdinand Stevens announced he was planning to take the unheard-of step of prosecuting owners of buildings where saloons were harbored.

Meanwhile, an unnamed deputy, possibly Stevens, threatened to use the nation's new Pure Food and Drug Act against the many dealers selling bad liquor. "It is the vilest, most evil liquid that man ever let burn his throat. A plain and criminal case of drugging," he charged.

A few days later, the deputies took on the "express companies," one of the many clever stratagems devised to flout prohibition. Using names like the Portsmouth & Bangor Express Company, these newly formed corporations ordered liquor legally under federal law from out-of-state mail-order distributors for customers' private use. But they were known to sell stored up goods illegally under state law to anyone who walked in.

The mayhem reached a high point late on the evening of August 29 when twenty Sturgis men surrounded some tenement buildings, including the Glenwood Hotel, on Harlow Street. Hundreds gathered in the street to watch the festivities. "The tenderloin was in a turmoil," chortled the *Bangor Daily News*.

The deputies approached the buildings in squads "like well-trained soldiers." Doors were smashed and windows broken. Once inside, the Sturgis men worked with surgical precision, moving from room to room "to the accompaniment of hysterical laughter, smothered screams and muttered curses." As lights began to flash on throughout the buildings, "white-gowned feminine figures flittered before the windows to the edification of the gaping crowd in the street below." Nothing was seized.

The raids knew no boundaries. Several other hostelries, including the Windsor Hotel, the Globe Hotel and the Aroostook House, were targeted. Even the Bangor House, the city's finest, lost its barkeep in a raid. Nor were the social clubs off limits (except the exclusive Tarratine). On September 14, the deputies raided the Bangor and Orono aeries of the Fraternal Order of Eagles, rummaging through the members' private lockers and hauling away wagonloads while onlookers threw mud and stones.

No dealer was too insignificant. Much of the liquor trade had moved into the streets. Richard A. Lamb, allegedly a pocket peddler, was arrested after he leaned over to pat a dog and a "long-necker" was observed protruding from his hip pocket. At the Eastern Maine State Fair, a man was arrested for selling ten-cent sips through a tube stretching from a bottle hidden in his coat.

Just what did all these strong-arm tactics accomplish? Not much if one counted up the drunks still on the street. Nearly a month after the raids had begun, on September 15, drunken men still roamed Exchange, Broad and Front Streets, reported a *Bangor Daily News* editorial. The next weekend, the paper reported that thirty men were arrested for intoxication. "The arrival of the Sturgis deputies…has changed the Bangor dealers' methods of effecting sales…but so far as reducing the amount of liquor sold in Bangor, the deputies have made small change," chided the newspaper, which supported prohibition as long as Bangoreans were left in control.

LIQUOR AMENDMENT SURVIVES REFERENDUM, BUT NOT IN BANGOR

September 5, 2011

A century ago next week, Mainers went to the polls to approve a direct primary law allowing them to vote for the nomination of political party candidates in primary elections, including seats in the U.S. Senate and

House and the state legislature. Democracy was on the march. But did anyone care much back then? The issue received little discussion in the newspapers compared to another question on the ballot—the state's notorious liquor laws.

Maine was famous for passing the first prohibition law in the nation in 1851. It was known nationally as the Maine Law. Thirty-three years later, in 1884, Mainers engraved it in legal concrete by inserting a prohibition amendment in the state's constitution. Now, in 1911, voters were being asked if they wanted to repeal the amendment.

The results of this referendum on election day, September 11, demonstrated that the rock-ribbed State of Maine was going soft on prohibition. Although the vote narrowly favored keeping the amendment, the numbers showed the Pine Tree State was now divided down the middle politically into two Maines—one wet and one dry. Wet Maine was getting bigger, while dry Maine remained barely in charge.

Even if the constitutional amendment had gone down in defeat, the law in the statute books prohibiting liquor sales would have continued to exist unless the legislature repealed or changed it. Supporters of the amendment, however, feared the law would be repealed or watered down if the amendment was repealed.

Many repeal advocates supported changing the law to "local option," which would allow towns or counties to decide for themselves if liquor would be sold. This change could not be made by the legislature as long as the amendment existed.

People opposed to state prohibition, including most Democrats and a growing number of "wet" Republicans, had wanted to repeal the amendment for decades. An effort by "dry" Republicans to enforce the law by creating an unpopular cadre of state liquor detectives (called the Sturgis Commission) had only riled up more opposition. The anger had helped Democrats seize the governor's office and both houses of the legislature in the last election. The stage was set in 1911 for a major test of state prohibition, but only if the amendment was defeated.

After sixty years, it was clear that the Maine Law was ineffective. Bangor in particular lacked the willpower to enforce it, in part because of the thousands of loggers and other transients who congregated there seasonally, and the many people who made money from their presence, including the rich property owners who leased space for saloons, seedy boardinghouses and the like.

Dozens of Bangor opinion leaders weighed in pro and con on whether to repeal the amendment. One of the most thoughtful was the Reverend

Charles Cutler, pastor of the First Congregational Church. He supported prohibition, but only if it were tied to the local option route. The current law promoted "lawlessness" and eroded self-government, he said in the *Bangor Daily Commercial* on September 6. In effect, Maine already had "lawless local option" because local law enforcement officials, including judges, decided for themselves whether to enforce the law, said Cutler.

The current system resulted in "spasms of enforcement" that drove the problem underground, resulting in pocket peddlers, drinking clubs and "dives...in every dark corner." Cutler also targeted the infamous Bangor Plan, under which anyone could sell liquor as long as he followed certain rules such as curfews and paid a small fine each year. (This system, as reflected in newspaper accounts, seemed to come and go with the political breezes.)

Frank Davis, Bangor's new police chief, continued enforcing the liquor law in Bangor in the same haphazard way as his predecessors right up until election day. He declared that barrooms must close at 10:00 p.m. Monday through Saturday and all day Sunday, it was announced on April 10 in the *Bangor Daily News*. That included "all-night restaurants" with a "bar annex." This arrangement antagonized some looking for a drink late at night, and "those who were real thirsty had to hunt around as much as 10 minutes before they could find anything," the *Bangor Daily News* reported sarcastically on April 13.

Davis and his men conducted a few raids singling out operators like Pope McKinnon and Billy Townsend, who were favorite targets. Another such victim, Hugh Jameson, was erecting a "handsome new saloon" on Harlow Street. Jameson's place, "resplendent in mahogany and glass," was raided on August 30 and again on September 9, yet he was still able to open for business "shortly after the raid...there apparently being sufficient stock left over to supply the trade."

Meanwhile, the results of the statewide vote on September 11 proved a surprise to many. The amendment was retained statewide by a slim majority of fewer than 800 out of more than 120,000 votes cast. While prohibition still ruled, its dominance appeared shaky and segregated mainly to rural areas. In most cities, repeal won by a landslide.

Bangoreans endorsed repeal by a three-to-one margin. The newspapers noted that, unlike in past elections, liquor and money to buy votes was absent at polling places. Also, many female temperance advocates, representing such groups as the Women's Christian Temperance Union, lobbied voters with signs and personal appeals even though they couldn't vote.

Once again, the old saying "As Maine goes, so goes the nation" held true. Many other states were jumping on the prohibition bandwagon that Maine had started rolling sixty years ago. In just a few years, federal Prohibition would add a whole new layer of confusion to the effort to control demon rum.

"OUR CITY—ITS PRIDE AND SHAME"

December 26, 2011

"Our City—Its Pride and Shame." That was the title of the Reverend Christopher W. Collier's sermon at the Hammond Street Congregational Church a century ago on Sunday morning, November 19, 1911. Being one of the most prominent clerics in the Queen City and given the importance of his subject, Collier had a ready audience. The *Bangor Daily News* published his words the next day.

Bangor's "pride," according to the Reverend Collier, was its wealth, its beauty and its generosity to the poor. Its shame was its failure to enforce the state's prohibition law. Just two months before, the state's voters had narrowly turned down an effort to repeal the prohibition amendment in the Maine constitution. Bangor voters, however, had voted by a three-to-one margin for repeal. This lopsided vote reflected the fact the city had not made a serious effort to enforce the liquor law in many years.

The Reverend Collier said he had traveled the world and seen the way laws were enforced in many countries. He declared he had "never in any land in any city...seen such callousness over violated law as I see every day here. It is enough to make every patriotic citizen blush with mortification and shame."

He had recently asked a number of "earnest men" how many saloons there were in Bangor. "One said 175, another said 300, another said, 'I don't know, but so far as the enforcement of the law is concerned, I don't see why there might not as well be 500 or 1,000.'"

"Can any lover of the city look on the saloons at the foot of Broad Street, at the head of Union Street, or those gathered around Pickering Square, all in open violation of the law, can he look on these and others like these and then speak of his city with pride?" the Reverend Collier wanted to know.

While the Reverend Collier was blushing in mortification, Police Chief Frank Davis, a man well grounded in the politics of the city, was planning his next liquor raids. These raids by Davis and former chiefs had for years been carefully crafted to make it look as though the city was trying to enforce prohibition when, in fact, it was regulating the steady flow of demon rum on its own terms and reaping some of the profits. Liquor dealers who followed local rules were left alone, but a few troublemakers were punished.

Back in April, Davis had made it clear that saloons would be allowed to operate if they followed certain standards. They had to close by 10:00 p.m. Monday through Saturday and shut down all day on Sundays. Davis's approach appeared to some to be a "renaissance of the Bangor Plan," the system under which hundreds of saloons flourished as long as they paid the city a fine each year.

The week after the Reverend Collier's sermon, and perhaps in reaction to it, Davis added a new wrinkle to his campaign. He targeted "kitchen barrooms," which operated on the lower end of the liquor hierarchy below the fancy saloons and hotel bars but a notch above "pocket peddlers," those fast-moving fellows who sold drinks in alleys or crowds from bottles concealed in the deep pockets of their coats. Kitchen bars were small-time, hole-in-the-wall operations. Because they were difficult to control, or even detect, they were especially anathema to the police and politicians who ran the city.

In what the *Bangor Daily News* declared to be the "largest raid ever made by the police department," Davis's men seized five "wagon and dray loads" of liquor at the Pickering Square cigar shop and May Street storehouse of James J. McCann on the Wednesday after the Reverend Collier's sermon. The haul included "18 barrels of ale, 19 halves of ale and 10 halves of lager." Instead of fighting the case the way most liquor dealers had been doing the past few years, McCann paid a fine of $100 and costs and presumably went right back into business.

The most interesting part of the story, however, was that McCann had been targeted—not because he was a liquor dealer but because he supplied kitchen barrooms.

"Kitchen Bars to be Wiped Out," declared a big headline in the *Bangor Daily News* on November 23, the day after the raid. A subhead declared, "Some Plain Talk by Chief Davis—Wholesalers Who Sell to Kitchen Bars Will Get Into Trouble."

"You may make this as plain as you like," Chief Davis told the newspaper reporter. "I intend to drive the kitchen bars out of business. They sell at all hours of the day and night, they are open Sundays and many of them dispense rank poison in place of liquor. In short, they are unmitigated evils, breeding all manner of lawlessness and crime, and I will not tolerate them."

McCann had violated his "explicit orders" not to sell to kitchen bars, declared Davis. The only evidence of this that the reporter could muster for his story was that McCann was alleged to have sold liquor to Mrs. Florence McNeil, a kitchen bar operator whose establishment had been raided the night before.

Davis, who spent much of his career working for city newspapers, had a way with words. He made it sound as if he was enforcing prohibition when in reality he was only nibbling around the edges of the Queen City's massive liquor trade. Too many people were profiting from demon rum for any official to make a serious effort to enforce the law. For the time being, the Reverend Collier and other law-abiding citizens would have to be satisfied until the political winds shifted in a drier direction.

Chapter 7

THE PROGRESSIVE ERA

THREE BANGOR REFORMERS

April 4, 2011

The Queen City of the East was flowering in reform efforts in the spring of 1911 as the Progressive Era bloomed across America. Some groups like the Anti-Saloon League and the Anti-Tuberculosis Association had specific agendas. Others, like the Twentieth Century Club, an organization of young businessmen, picked their battles, from the enforcement of prostitution laws to advocacy of a law banning public drinking cups in schools. Immigrants, loggers, juvenile delinquents, unwed mothers and paupers all had their advocates, while public institutions like the jail and the poorhouse were targeted for improvements.

Jane Addams, Jacob Riis, Booker T. Washington and other nationally known reformers gave lectures in Bangor. Local leaders also emerged onto the crowded public stage. They included ministers and professors, clubwomen and even an occasional politician. This column is about three such local individuals whose advocacy received extensive coverage in the Bangor newspapers.

The Reverend Charles H. Cutler of the First Congregational Church called for an end to "inhuman" conditions at the Penobscot County Jail after walking through the institution. His Sunday sermon on the subject

Professor Robert J. Sprague of the University of Maine was one of the leading voices for reform in Bangor during the Progressive Era. *Courtesy of the University of Maine Special Collections.*

was published in part in Bangor's two daily newspapers on October 31, 1910. "SHOCKING CONDITIONS IN THE BANGOR JAIL," shouted the headline in the *Bangor Daily News*. "Womanhood Degraded and Young Men Exposed to Evil Influence."

The jail was grossly overcrowded. Boys were put in cells with hardened criminals. Women's quarters were too close to the men's, and there was no female jail attendant. 140 prisoners were crowded into a space built for 70. "In cells designed for two men, five were now sleeping, with barely room enough in the space eight feet square for five mattresses. Each cell, [Cutler] said, is lighted by one small, barred window in the corridor, is very poorly ventilated, and with scarcely any sanitary conveniences whatever."

"Sanitary facilities" in the cells consisted of "small pails," according to another story about the findings of a state prison inspector published in the *Bangor Daily Commercial* on November 7. There was no mention of running water, which was still a luxury in many homes.

Many of those incarcerated had been convicted only of drunkenness, by far the most common crime of the era, or no crime at all. Some were in jail because they could not pay bail or because they were being held as witnesses.

Another crusading Bangor minister was the Reverend Alva Roy Scott of the Unitarian Church. "MAKE BANGOR THE CLEANEST CITY!" he exhorted from the pulpit, according to the *Bangor Daily News* on March 27, 1911. That was the way to fight tuberculosis and other ills.

Scott's target was Bangor's "bad housing which tends to impair the physical or moral health of the tenant; where there is lack of water drainage or sewage; where the yards are...sodden, foul smelling; where old suds and dishwater stand in slimy pools; where there are ashes piled up, garbage and rubbish and decayed outbuildings."

Like the Reverend Cutler, the Reverend Scott had done some sleuthing. "I am convinced by frequent tramps through all parts of the city that there is more unfit housing than most of us are aware. Not far off is a street with a row of houses fairly well built, ashes and rubbish, old barrels and cultch are in front crowding upon the sidewalk. Children are playing here and tracking indoors...." Most of the inhabitants were immigrants. Scott believed that "every child brought up in an unfit tenement is a probable consumptive and a possible pauper or criminal." He seemed more interested in the yards around these tenements than in their interiors.

One could almost call Robert J. Sprague, a professor of economics and sociology at the University of Maine, a professional reformer, so broad were his interests and so frequently were his opinions printed in the Bangor newspapers. In pieces in the *Bangor Daily News* on December 7, 1910, and the *Commercial* on March 2, 1911, he proposed a wide-ranging reform agenda for the state of Maine for the next ten years leading up to the centennial of its statehood in 1920. Beautification of country homes, school and church yards, railroad stations and town centers was high on his list, with the planting of trees and bushes a top priority. Not only would they improve the looks of the barren wastelands that characterized many communities, but they would also protect people from the clouds of dust containing dried horse dung, tuberculosis germs and other noxious substances believed to reside in the dirt roads of the day.

Clearing the streets was another of Sprague's priorities. "Grocers and other merchants often dump piles of boxes, barrels, paper and other waste beside their buildings, disfiguring the street and scattering rubbish. Cordwood is often piled along the village streets and old burned trees and debris is often allowed to lie around for months or years after a village fire," said the professor.

Sprague also targeted "hideous" roadside advertising, idle jail prisoners, the lack of vocational education ("schools of enginry," where students could learn how to service the new gas-powered engines), dirt sidewalks, rutted roads, unhealthy drinking water that caused typhoid and more.

"The state has much to say about what the people will not drink but does not make much provision for what it shall drink. For everyone that dies of alcoholism, 25 die of typhoid," noted Dr. Sprague. Such were conditions in Bangor and other cities back in the "good old days."

CHARITIES SOUGHT TO HELP WOODSMEN

March 21, 2011

The logging crews were starting to arrive from the woods, announced the *Bangor Daily Commercial* on March 10 a century ago. "Every day brings a bunch of them, and within a week, the usual spring quota of log handlers will have arrived in Bangor to pass a lazy three weeks while awaiting the drives," wrote the reporter sent to cover this important annual event, which swelled the population of the Queen City of the East by several thousand.

Soon many of these men would be hustling about from one employment agency to another hunting for jobs on the river drives. Many would be spending their money on flophouses, bootleg liquor and women of questionable virtue. Many would be broke within a short time, and not a few would end up in jail for drunkenness or worse. Some would fail to get river-driving jobs, which tended to go to experienced men. They might end up stranded in Bangor or forced to become hoboes, riding the rails out of town.

While that's all true, it's not the whole story. The Progressive Era was well underway in 1911. Upright citizens wanted to help the downtrodden rise out of poverty and spiritual degradation. The Young Men's Christian Association and the Salvation Army were among the groups in the vanguard of this movement. They wanted to protect loggers and other transient workers from what the *Bangor Daily News* described on April 12 as "40 gambling places and 200 saloons running practically day and night" and from "the army of procurers and scarlet women who subsist in large measure from the visitors' rather guileless innocence."

The paper went on to describe the situation as "a cheap, tawdry, stupid, but powerful and well-organized octopus of crime, unhampered to any noticeable extent by public officials in high places." Such unusually blunt language in the *Bangor Daily News* was a sure sign that the Progressive Era had overtaken the Queen City.

The Bangor YMCA that season leased a small store with "a long, low-ceilinged room" on Washington Street across from the train station, in the heart of the district frequented by loggers, where it started a "club room for woodsmen." It was intended to replace the religious meetings that had been held on an experimental basis that winter at Sam Golden's nearby employment agency.

The YMCA's "reading room" was described in detail by the *Commercial* on March 29. "Men Wanted" read a sign over the door. These men were

The employment agency run by Sam Golden and Charles Largay was a landmark for unemployed woodsmen. *Courtesy of Richard R. Shaw.*

invited to read newspapers and magazines, play games or just relax and have a smoke. Meetings were held each evening, and coffee and doughnuts were served at Sunday religious services.

During one such meeting at Golden's a few weeks before, fifty men had attended. Fourteen were found to be "worthy of aid. They were young men mostly who found themselves in Bangor without a cent and who would not beg. They were also given dinner at the YMCA building, the meal costing $1," said the newspaper. They were promised a place to sleep "if they manifested an inclination to seek work. The men are not generally down and out, simply stranded here in Bangor for a short time, and needing a place to stay."

This was back in the days before public homeless shelters, when welfare was chiefly a private endeavor and philanthropic organizations spent a great deal of time pondering whether a recipient was a member of the "deserving poor" or the "undeserving poor." Bangor was a great hobo center then, and it was believed some of the men who passed through town on the trains had no interest in working.

The new Washington Street room was placed in charge of W.J. Miller, "lumberman's secretary of the Maine YMCA." He had been traveling from one lumber camp to another during the winter. He was assisted by James Potvin, "who has been at work in the woods and saved his funds instead of spending them all as he formerly did."

One goal was to get the men to contact their relatives. A sign on the wall asked, "When did you write home last?" A writing desk was provided with free pen, ink and paper. "Many men are ignorant of the ways of telegraphing for money and otherwise communicating with friends or relatives when broke," said the newspaper.

If this experiment worked, YMCA officials planned to install beds so some hard-luck cases could spend the night. But the Salvation Army had an even bigger idea. Fundraising for a "workingman's hotel" had begun a couple of years ago. The Reverend Frederic Palladino gave a talk at City Hall on November 6, 1910, describing the conditions that made such a workingman's hotel necessary. 1,200 members of the city's Protestant churches attended. "Through [the Reverend Palladino's] eyes, they saw conditions, to many only dimly realized, in all their ugly truthfulness—the swarms of woodsmen alighting at the [train] station, turned loose upon the city with but few protecting hands to guide them from the obvious evils which await at every turn," the *Bangor Daily News* reported.

As many as five thousand woodsmen passed through Bangor each year. "We can't dodge the main issue," said the minister. "We can't lay back and say,

'Let this element be isolated and we will enjoy our fine homes undisturbed.' These isolated sections [of the city], if they foster their own vices and set their own standards of morality, will become festering sores."

Many of these men were already "settled in viciousness," but an even larger number, unskilled and often ignorant, were honest men who needed help—and, of course, religious conversion.

"I wish you could stand with me someday in the Union Station and see the Aroostook trains come in—could see these hundreds upon hundreds of visitors stream from the cars into Exchange Street and into the city's life," said the Reverend Palladino. "They have no homes, no friends, yet they knock for admission at our gates."

Four years later, the Salvation Army dedicated its new headquarters and "workingman's hotel" at 55 York Street. Several decades later, after the passing of the "swarms of woodsmen," it was demolished as part of Urban Renewal.

FIRST PUBLIC PLAYGROUND

July 7, 2008

A campaign to build public playgrounds for city children was sweeping the nation at the turn of the twentieth century. Bangor became part of the movement on July 6, 1908, a century ago this week, when the city's first public playground opened in Abbott Square on Harlow Street next to what was then Bangor High School. "For Bangor, the thing is very much of an experiment," said the *Bangor Daily News* on the morning after the grand opening. "The matter has been agitated for a long time, and the conclusion was finally reached that something ought to be done about it."

The Abbott Square playground would be open to boys aged ten or under and girls aged twelve or under from 9:00 a.m. to 11:30 a.m. and 1:00 p.m. to 3:00 p.m. The city had provided the space and a salary for a trained playground supervisor. The equipment was purchased by private donations. Anyone who wanted to contribute could leave his money at Merrill Trust Company. Dr. W.C. Peters and the Reverend Charles H. Cutler of the First Congregational Society were identified as the leaders in the local movement.

Miss Caroline Besarick of Dorchester, Massachusetts, had been hired as playground superintendent. She was a graduate of Boston Normal School of Gymnastics, and she had run playgrounds and taught physical education in Boston and elsewhere. She was portrayed in the newspapers as energetic, personable and fully capable of commanding the attention and respect of the 125 to 150 children who were in attendance on average during the first two weeks. It was important that she create a good impression. Advocates were already calling for the creation of more playgrounds at a time when various groups were clamoring for a new public library, a bridge over the Kenduskeag Stream to the new train station and other improvements.

Both of the city's daily newspapers sent reporters to observe activities at the Abbott Square playground. "One hundred and fifteen children were scattered about the yard playing at the different games and enjoying themselves to their heart's content," reported the *Bangor Daily Commercial* on the afternoon of the opening. "Swings, sand boxes, tennis and jack straws were occupying the attention of the children, and in a day or two, there will be ready for use tether ball, high jumping, running courses and basketball. For this last game baskets have been ordered and when received will be placed at the proper height on the two large elms in the upper end of the yard." Tennis was "modified," allowing eight children to play at once.

The *Bangor Daily News* reporter pronounced the playground an instant success. It had "demonstrated its usefulness before it had been open an hour," he wrote. One of its youthful male attendees told the reporter that first morning from his sand box perch, "Sure I likes it. And youse kin bet I'm comin' termorrer and ev're day."

Under Miss Besarick's tutelage, by the second week of the playground's existence, the girls were enjoying "mock teas" (with toy dishes but no tea), while the boys were participating in field days with running and other competitive events. But the large sandboxes—ten feet square with three-foot-high sides with a shelf—remained the favorite spot to be. Each child was supplied with a pail and a small shovel.

Public playgrounds, as envisioned by social reformers, were not merely for entertainment and exercise. America was beset by extreme poverty. A flood of immigrants added to the problem daily. Playgrounds were seen as a way to socialize children—to show them how democracy worked (or what we might call sharing and teamwork today) through experience rather than abstract instruction.

Miss Besarick was well aware of this important social role. The new playground had been advertised only in the newspapers. She told the *Commercial* on opening day that she was planning to visit as many families as possible who didn't read newspapers to get them to send their children. "I wish we could get hold of more poor children," she told a *Bangor Daily News* reporter for the July 11 issue. "The little ones we have here now are dears, but I'd like to see the poorer ones coming. That is really what a playground is for. Everything is delightfully satisfactory as it is, and we really are doing splendid work. But we want to get hold of the poorest of the poor."

She continued, "No, you haven't any slums in Bangor. You have light and air, and when you have those, you haven't slums. You have poverty, but you haven't any wretchedness and squalor. Not as wretchedness and squalor are classed in the tenement districts of the great cities."

Plans were afoot to build more playgrounds. The *Bangor Daily News* reported in the same story that an effort was underway to establish a duplicate playground near the river on Hancock Street near where many immigrants lived.

Meanwhile, the *Bangor Daily Commercial* was conducting a campaign to have a playground built in Chapin Park. All one had to do to understand the need was to observe recess at the nearby Palm Street School, where "400 boys are forced to seek their recreation in a yard that allows but two feet for each boy…packed in like sardines in a box. A similar situation prevails on the girls' side."

The toughest battle, however, over whether city playgrounds were a useful contribution to the community, had already been won. More were on the way. They would become a permanent fixture in Bangor, thanks to the small group of people who fought for them a century ago.

SCHOOL FOR IMMIGRANTS

February 2, 2009

The new immigrants flooding the nation a century ago were greeted with trepidation even as their services on construction gangs were welcomed in Bangor and other cities. Newspapers summed up many of the fears. "INFLOW OF ALIENS MENACE TO NATION," declared a front-page headline in the *Bangor Daily Commercial* on January 7, 1907. A former Cornell University professor urged that all American college students be given military instruction to cope with the disorder and rebellion that was surely coming.

That was only one of the many stories expressing fears and contempt for the great influx of foreigners. Whenever a fight broke out or a petty theft was committed on Bangor's Hancock Street, the center of the city immigrant population, it was sure to make headlines. Often, courtroom interpreters were required as well as lawyers to settle these disputes.

A sure way to tame this tidal wave of humanity was to Americanize it, believed the most progressive citizens. Before this could happen, the newcomers needed to learn how to speak English. A century ago, efforts were underway in Bangor to make sure this would occur.

The YMCA planned to employ "college men" from the University of Maine to teach English and possibly basic arithmetic at night in a room in the former York Street School. "There are hundreds of foreign-speaking men in Bangor, the larger percent of them being Italians and Russian Jews," noted the *Bangor Daily Commercial* in a story on November 5, 1908. No mention was made of women.

The idea was not new in Bangor. Previous efforts had been made to start such a school at the YMCA building. "They were somewhat diffident about coming to the association building, where there were always many young men in better circumstances than theirs, and for this reason, the YMCA decided to go to them," the story reported.

Another story on November 11 announced that a school for Italians—a Union Mission school—was also in the planning stages. E.A. Natino of Springfield, Massachusetts, a native of Venice, was in Bangor to generate interest. The *Commercial* story reported that Natino had been engaged in Salvation Army work in New York City and had much experience in founding such schools. Natino said there were about one hundred Italians living in Bangor. I did not see any further notice of this effort in the Bangor newspapers.

The YMCA night school started sometime in late November or December. The *Commercial* declared it a success on January 1, 1909. An average of twenty-five students, "all Hebrews," were attending the classes three times a week. Their average age was thirty. The head teacher was University of Maine law school student Harry Sacknoff, son of a Portland rabbi. Two fellow students, Joseph Druker and Stephen Brady, were his assistants. They taught reading, writing and spelling.

The education of women also was mentioned. "There have been a number of inquiries made at the YMCA concerning a school for girls run on the same principle. Many of the Hebrew girls of the city who have passed the public school age are desirous of seeing such a class formed."

Such a school was founded the second week in January, the *Commercial* announced on January 30. Organized by Miss Mary Spratt, "one of Bangor's progressive and earnest teachers," the class met Monday, Tuesday

The Valentine School, located at Union and First Streets, hosted one of the earliest classes for adult immigrants in Bangor. Today, the building is the Shaw House, a shelter for teenagers. *Courtesy of Richard R. Shaw.*

and Thursday evenings at the Valentine School at Union and First Streets. Twenty-one women, mostly "Syrians, Hebrews and others who are of such an age or so employed that attendance upon our public schools is not practicable for them," attended to learn English and arithmetic.

The schoolroom was provided by the school board, while the King's Daughters' Union, the Athene Club and some individuals had donated money for expenses. The students still had to pay ten cents per class. Miss Spratt's assistant was Miss Helen Christian of the city's teacher training class.

Eventually these night schools were absorbed by the public school system, which was already educating hundreds of foreign-speaking children. A night school was established at Bangor High School by the school board in the 1914–15 school year.

Over the years, Miss Spratt's name became closely associated with her efforts to teach young immigrant children at the State Street School, where more than half the enrollment was foreign born, as well as with the earliest night school classes. She described her work in a speech to the Bangor Chamber of Commerce reported in the *Commercial* on May 29, 1920. The reporter wrote, "It is estimated during the last 15 years perhaps, 2,000 little foreigners have been taught to speak the first English words they knew" at the school, and a great many adults had been taught at the night school started some thirteen years before. The effort represented "Americanization in the biggest and best sense of the word."

In outlining her philosophy, Miss Spratt told the local businessmen, "There is no way by which we can make anyone feel that it is a blessed and splendid thing to be an American, unless we ourselves are aglow with the sacred fire—unless we interpret Americanism by our kindness, our courage, our generosity and our fairness." In this way, an older generation of Bangoreans helped create a new one in spite of all the fears and prejudices that had to be overcome.

VOTERS' LEAGUE DEMANDED MORAL REFORM

April 6, 2009

"SCARLET LADIES; FLOODS OF RUM." This bold lead on a multi-tiered headline at the top of page one of the *Bangor Daily News* on Monday morning April 5, 1909, was a shocker even for the Queen City. It continued, "Surprising Conditions Discussed as Mayor and Police Chief Face Broadside of Questions From the Voters' League."

Proper Bangoreans were fed up with vice, and they weren't going to take it any more. The Voters' League was the latest manifestation of the Progressive Era in Bangor. Reform was in the breeze, and city fathers had better take a sniff.

They appeared to have gotten the message already.

The weekend before this momentous meeting among the Voters' League, the mayor and the police chief, Bangor cops had rounded up a dozen streetwalkers, or "lady friends," as they were sometimes known. Liquor raids had been on tap as well.

"Whether Chief Bowen wants to make a record as a reformer or whether he thought it was about time to make a demonstration to frighten the bar keepers and the women, nobody knows," commented a surprised reporter for the *Bangor Daily News* on March 29.

The upstanding men of the Voters' League were not so easily impressed, however. A special committee, consisting of "preachers, substantial businessmen, eminent representatives of many professions and trades," came to City Hall on Saturday night, April 3, for separate meetings with Mayor John F. Woodman and Chief of Police John C. Bowen. They asked, "Why are some of the laws here enforced and others nullified? Why do hundreds of bad women parade the streets at night, and why do hundreds of saloons run wide open day and night? Why is Bangor sometimes quoted as one of the wickedest... cities of its size in New England? Why are the police so blind to so many things?"

Mayor Woodman was a model host. He brought forth a bag of large oranges and a box of choice cigars. He smiled graciously. He shook hands. He greeted many of the petitioners by their first names. He was completely non-committal. "Gentlemen, I will take under consideration all that you have said," he repeated.

Prohibition had existed in Maine for more than fifty years, yet one could still obtain a drink in the best hotels or the lowest dives. Prostitutes plied their trade openly, and slot machines sat on the counters of untold numbers of businesses. This circus of vice was propped up especially at this time of year by the thousands of loggers, sailors and other transient laborers passing through the city.

Police Chief John C. Bowen. *Courtesy of the Bangor Museum and History Center.*

Mayor John E. Woodman. *Courtesy of the Bangor Museum and History Center.*

147

Attempts at law enforcement were sporadic. The police rounded up the usual suspects and seized a few gallons of booze when political conditions were ripe. Under the city's infamous "Bangor Plan," liquor dealers were fined instead of jailed, and the money was used for civic betterment projects.

Bangor's reputation as a vice capital grew as the state's legislature fumbled. "BANGOR NOT DRY; 300 PLACES OPEN," a large, embarrassing front-page headline in the *Bangor Daily News* on February 20 had declared based on the testimony of a senator from nearby Knox County who wanted to resubmit prohibition to the state's voters. Meanwhile, Maine's governor that year vetoed a bill that would have made jail sentences mandatory for liquor violators.

"For the second city of the state, in wealth and population, to nullify the constitution of the state and refuse to enforce its laws, is a simple case of anarchy," Professor Robert Sprague of the University of Maine told Mayor Woodman on that Saturday evening when the Voters' League took on City Hall. Nobody seemed to know who was responsible for enforcing the laws, and Woodman did little to clarify the issue.

Hadn't the chief of police declared that liquor would not be sold on Sundays or after 10:00 p.m., implying that its sale was sanctioned at other times, asked Edgar M. Simpson, a lawyer? "Could you find outside the libretto of a comic opera anything more exquisitely ridiculous?" The Reverend Frederick Palladino of the Pine Street Methodist Church added, "If a man wants liquor here, he can get enough of it to swim in. The city is wider open now than it was last fall. More drunken men are staggering in the streets. A short time ago, I made an investigation of the boardinghouse district, and of the 60 places which I visited, liquor could be had in 40."

Professor Sprague had done his own investigation, noting:

Recently, I entered one of the leading hotels of this city. On the left of the smoking room, there were three men lying flat on the floor in a drunken stupor. On the right, there were four others in the same condition. Three more were laid out dead to the world on chairs. I passed into the bar. Seventeen men were drinking beer and whiskey. On my way out, I passed a policeman who was walking comfortably back and forth before the door. There is no place in this country…where you find more degenerate holes than in the city of Bangor. Are the police blind—or are they told to be blind?

The Reverend Carl F. Henry of the Universalist Church asserted Bangor's reputation was blocking national reform:

A vast sentiment of moral reform, a great wave of prohibition, is sweeping over the country. And do you know the chief obstacle to this countrywide sweep of civic advancement? It is the city of Bangor! The utter failure of prohibition in this one city is quoted from the Atlantic to the Pacific, from the Great Lakes to the Gulf. It has defeated wholesome legislation as far away as the state of Washington. It has worked incalculable harm.

After this lopsided exchange, the Voters' League moved downstairs to grill Police Chief Bowen. Not surprisingly, the police had just completed another raid. Billy Townsend's unsavory roadhouse on Stillwater Avenue had been roughed up a bit. The results were in plain view as the men from the Voters' League entered the police station. "They found the office filled with somewhat tousled, peevish ladies, four-gallon jugs of whiskey and innumerable glasses with foamy suds still lingering in their depths," reported the *Bangor Daily News*.

How seriously would these respectable gentlemen of the Voters' League be taken as the days went by? We can get some small idea by moving ahead to a meeting of the common council reported in the *Bangor Daily News* on April 14. Councilman Benjamin W. Blanchard read an order calling on the chief of police to enforce prohibition more stringently. Councilors looked surprised as if Blanchard "had exploded a dynamite bomb instead of a verbal one."

"Is it necessary," asked Councilman John H. Fahey, jumping to his feet, "to instruct the chief of police to do his duty? I move that the order be laid on the table."

"Under the table," suggested Councilman Patrick O'Leary.

"This isn't the Voters' League," remarked someone else.

Blanchard "started to walk from his seat to the president's desk, and long before he reached it, the order was as dead as a door nail. It had been tabled promptly, unanimously, and amid rounds of derisive laughter."

Boy Scouts' First Hike

June 21, 2010

From the Boy Scouts to the Moral Muscle League, clubs for boys were on the upswing a century ago as reformers looked for ways to keep young men on the straight and narrow. Bangor's new playground promoters and the YMCA seemed to be behind much of the activity in the Queen City.

The old Bangor YMCA building. *Courtesy of Richard R. Shaw.*

Bangor's newest playground director, Miss Susan Myers, got right to work founding three clubs in the city's poorest neighborhoods for boys ages ten to sixteen after she was hired in the spring of 1910. One met at the Valentine schoolhouse on First Street, drawing many of its members from the Devil's Half-Acre area, said the *Bangor Daily News* on April 12. A second, named the United States Club, met at the Pine Street School, attracting small boys from upper York and Hancock Streets, an area heavily populated by immigrants. A third club met at Abbott Square, site of the city's first public playground and the location of the high school, across from where the Bangor Public Library is today. Each club met one night a week and was staffed by two volunteers. The boys' activities included saluting the flag and performing gymnastics. Then they played games and had an occasional boxing match. Baseball was a major pastime as well. "Just how enthusiastic the boys are may be imagined when the fact is known that last week Miss Myers was called from her dinner to the door to be confronted by two small boys who explained that they were the captain and manager of a ball team and wanted to know if they could be in one of the clubs with the rest of the [team]," reported the newspaper.

A club for girls was also meeting at the Bangor Theological Seminary, according to the newspaper two days later, although it certainly wasn't getting as much publicity as the boys' activities.

The next big news about Bangor clubs for boys came two months later. "BOY SCOUTS HERE," announced a headline in the *Bangor Daily Commercial* on June 21. "The Boy Scout movement, which has spread like wildfire over England and which has already gained much headway in the United States, has reached Bangor. Ass't. Sec. James B. Withee, who has charge of the boy's department at the YMCA, is organizing a scout group, and they will shortly become affiliated with the Boy Scouts of America."

At least one local Boy Scout troop had already been assembled the previous fall across the river in Brewer under the auspices of the Brewer Congregational Church and the Boy Scouts of England. Now that an American organization had been formed, troops were rapidly forming all over the nation.

The Bangor troop's first activity was a hike and camping trip. "They will leave the YMCA building at 7 o'clock Tuesday and will march over the country roads and fields to Levant, 10 miles distant," the *Commercial* explained. "The Boys' club of Levant will have tents pitched for them when they arrive, and they will camp there for a night. The return trip will be made Wednesday."

The campsite was going to be on Black Stream, the *Bangor Daily News* said three days later. "Those who attend are requested to wear khaki trousers, blue flannel shirt, slouch hat, red bandanna handkerchief and heavy shoes. Each scout must carry tin dipper, plate, knife, fork, spoon and single blanket." Those who wanted to make the trip were asked to call Mr. Withee at 329-11.

A dozen boys, each carrying a blanket roll over his shoulder, left on this expedition, the newspaper said on June 29. Lunch was to be cooked by the roadside at noon, and "one of the rules of the hike is that each scout shall cook his own meal." Keep in mind this was in the days before lightweight packs, freeze-dried food and other tools for making camping easy.

The list, or at least a partial list, of these original Bangor Boy Scouts, as published in the *Bangor Daily News* on June 29, is worth preserving here for the ages. They included Edgar Bowler, John Philbrook, Philip Howe, Leland Millett, Charles Shaw, Harold D. Banton, Joseph Murch, William E. Bass, Russell C. Foster, Frank A. Estes and Ralph Jordan. Anyone who has been a Boy Scout in a new troop and gone on the first hike and cooked his first meal outdoors knows about the excitement they felt.

THERE WILL NEVER BE ANOTHER JENNIE JOHNSON

April 27, 2009

If you were down and out in Bangor a century ago, you might get a visit from Mrs. Jennie Johnson, city missionary. She would want to check to see if you were one of the deserving poor (too sick to work, with a wife and kids) or the undeserving poor (too lazy or drunk to work). If you fell into the former category, she would then attend to your needs, offering you a new pair of shoes, a hot meal and some winter clothes—perhaps even a job. She couldn't provide you with a lot of money from government welfare programs because there weren't any.

Jennie Johnson's name was often in the newspapers. In the summer, she took an army of hooting and hollering kids to Riverside Park in Hampden on the trolley. At Christmas, she threw a Christmas party at City Hall for poor kids.

A look at her official report dated April 12, 1909, gives a clearer idea of what sort of operation she ran. "During the year I have made 796 calls upon

Jennie Johnson and her dog are seen here standing outside City Hall in the front row of a group of city employees in 1921. We can speculate today that the dog accompanied her on her many walks into dangerous neighborhoods to help the poor and ailing. *Courtesy of the Bangor Museum and History Center.*

poor persons and families and have distributed 293 pairs of shoes, 1,356 articles of clothing, much bedding and quantities of food and medicine," she wrote.

Most of the $463 she had available to spend came from the proceeds of the city's George Stetson fund and from the charity dance she organized each year. Money had also been donated by the Elks, Edward H. Blake and Mrs. H. C. Chapman. Food had been donated by Weferling's Restaurant and J.H. Snow & Company. Many unnamed individuals had also donated food and clothes.

Everyone loved and admired Jennie Johnson. Talk to the denizens of the city's slums, especially in Ward One along the riverfront, where many immigrants lived and the unemployed hung out, or to the police who solicited her help in dealing with abused children and injured women, or to the businessmen who contributed money to her cause. Jennie Johnson was an intrepid warrior. She certainly was no "kid glove woman," commented one supporter.

So what got her into so much political hot water in 1909? Was it new trends in social work? Or was it the fact she was a Catholic? I would guess it was some combination of the two.

The newspapers revealed the bare essentials of the power play to oust Mrs. Johnson on April 13, 1909. It appeared that the Twentieth Century Club, one of the city's leading progressive organizations, had hatched a plot to have her replaced by Mrs. Alva R. Scott, wife of the outspoken reform-minded minister of the Unitarian Church. A petition said what was needed was "a modern system of charity work whereby the best scientific, economic and cooperative methods may be employed." Mrs. Scott had "special technical training and a wide practical experience in such work." The five-member petition committee, which was working "under the auspices of the Twentieth Century Club," represented various charitable organizations of the city.

A story in the *Bangor Daily News* on May 14 was more explicit about the plot to oust Mrs. Johnson: "Certain people wanted to have the work under the supervision of a charity organization with one of their members as city missionary." This was all in keeping with certain trends current at the time tending toward the professionalization of social work and the centralization of welfare.

Jennie Johnson's religion, however, apparently had also been cited as a reason for change. "It has been reported that some persons, who in their efforts to have another appointed in the place of Mrs. Johnson, have said that she has been partial to Catholics, she being a member of the Catholic Church," the *Commercial* reported in its original story on April 13.

Jennie Johnson had many defenders. The most outspoken may have been Police Chief John C. Bowen, who said of her:

> *Mrs. Johnson is one of the most efficient city missionaries we have ever had. We have had occasion to send for her at all hours of the day and frequently at night, and she has always responded to our calls promptly and cheerfully. She has always been willing to go down into the slums….I don't believe there is another woman who would go where we have asked Mrs. Johnson to go.*

As the days went by, more people stepped forward to praise Mrs. Johnson. Among them was John L. Parker, formerly of the bankrupt shoe company Parker & Peakes, which was located in Ward One. "There are men in Bangor of the stamp who are not over-enthusiastic over charitable work who take off their hats every time to Mrs. Johnson," he said in the *Commercial* on April 14.

Two days later, Max Cohen, one of Bangor's Jewish leaders, testified to the high level of support Mrs. Johnson had among Jews, many of whom were recent immigrants.

A showdown before the Board of Aldermen occurred on May 13. City Solicitor Donald F. Snow delivered the opinion that the city had missed its opportunity to fire Mrs. Johnson and hire someone else. The ordinance said the appointment had to take place in March. The city would have to "show cause" if it wished to fire her now. Obviously, that would have been difficult to do considering the outpouring of support she had received. A committee was formed hastily to rewrite the ordinance.

I turned the clock ahead a few decades to ascertain the outcome of this political tiff. Jennie Johnson's obituary on May 25, 1950, provided the answer. At her death, she had been the city missionary for forty-five years until she had to step down because of illness. City Council Chairman Charles E. Sheehan summed up her life this way: "The citizens of Bangor have lost a truly fine friend and public official. Jennie Johnson was a very kind, thoughtful and charitable woman. She can never be replaced. There will never be another Jennie Johnson."

Selected Bibliography

Newspapers

Bangor Daily Commercial
Bangor Daily News
Industrial Journal

Books and Pamphlets

Angier, Jerry, and Herb Cleaves. *Bangor and Aroostook: The Maine Railroad.* Littleton, MA: Yankee Express Enterprises, 1986.

Barry, William David. *Maine: The Wilder Half of New England.* Gardiner, ME: Tilbury House, 2012.

Berlin, Marc, Ardeana Hamlin, Richard Shaw and Gig Weeks. *The Story of Bangor: A Brief History of Maine's Queen City.* Bangor, ME: BookMarc's Publishing, 1999.

Blanding, Edward Mitchell. *The City of Bangor.* Bangor, ME: Bangor Board of Trade, 1899.

SELECTED BIBLIOGRAPHY

Branniff, Linda K. *Bangor's Bijou and Mr. Bogrett: A History of the Early Years of the Bijou Theater*. Bangor, ME: L.K. Branniff, 2003.

Goldstein, Judith S. *Crossing Lines: Histories of Jews and Gentiles in Three Communities*. New York: Morrow, 1992.

Hatch, Louis C. *Maine: A History*. Somersworth, NH: New Hampshire Publishing Company, 1974. (Facsimile of 1919 edition.)

Heseltine, Charles D. *Bangor Street Railway*. Warehouse Point, CT: Connecticut Valley Chapter of the National Railway Historical Society, 1974.

Ives, Edward D. *Argyle Boom*. Orono, ME: Northeast Folklore Society, 1977.

Judd, Richard W., Edwin A. Churchill and Joel W. Eastman. *Maine: The Pine Tree State from Prehistory to the Present*. Orono: University of Maine Press, 1995.

Lee, Maureen Elgersman. *Black Bangor: African Americans in a Maine Community, 1880–1950*. Durham: University of New Hampshire Press, 2005.

Lunt, Dean Lawrence. *Here for Generations: The Story of a Maine Bank and Its City*. Frenchboro, ME: Islandport Press, 2002.

Price, H.H., and Gerald E. Talbot. *Maine's Visible Black History: The First Chronicle of Its People*. Gardiner, ME: Tilbury House, 2006.

Reilly, Wayne E. *Remembering Bangor: The Queen City Before the Great Fire*. Charleston, SC: The History Press, 2009.

Richardson, John Mitchell. *Steamboat Lore of the Penobscot: An Informal Story of Steamboating in Maine's Penobscot Region*. Augusta, ME: Kennebec Journal Print Shop, 1941.

Scee, Trudy Irene. *City on the Penobscot: A Comprehensive History of Bangor, Maine*. Charleston, SC: The History Press, 2010.

Scontras, Charles A. *Time-Line of Selected Highlights of Maine Labor History: 1636–2003*. Orono: Bureau of Labor Education, University of Maine, 2003.

SELECTED BIBLIOGRAPHY

Shaw, Richard R. *Bangor*. Augusta, ME: Alan Sutton Inc., 1994.

———. *Bangor in Vintage Postcards*. Charleston, SC: Arcadia Publishing, 2004.

Smith, David C. *A History of Lumbering in Maine, 1861–1960*. Orono: University of Maine Press, 1972.

Thompson, Deborah. *Bangor, Maine, 1769–1914: An Architectural History*. Orono: University of Maine Press, 1988.

Vickery, James B. *Made in Bangor: Economic Emergence and Adaptation, 1834–1911*. Bangor, ME: Bangor Historical Society, 1984.

Vickery, James B., ed. *Bangor, Maine: An Illustrated History*. Reprinted by Bangor Bi-Centennial Commission, n.d.

Wasson, George S. *Sailing Days on the Penobscot*. Salem, MA: Marine Research Society, 1932.

Zelz, Abigail Ewing, and Marilyn Zoidis. *Woodsmen and Whigs: Historic Images of Bangor, Maine*. Virginia Beach, VA: The Donning Company Publishers, 1991.

ARTICLES

Day, Holman. "Does Prohibition Pay? Maine After Fifty-seven Years of Prohibition." *Appleton's Magazine* (August, 1908): 183–90.

Reilly, Wayne E. "Eastern Maine—1900." *Bangor Daily News*, January 8, 2000.

———. "Ethnic Bangor: Rediscovering Our City's Past." *Bangor Daily News*, December 1–8, 2007.

Reilly, Wayne E., and Richard R. Shaw. "In Search of the Real Fan Jones," *Down East*, April 1988.

SELECTED BIBLIOGRAPHY

THESES

Banfield, Alfred T., Jr. "The History and Ethnicity of Italians in Maine." MA, Liberal Studies, University of Maine, 1989.

King, Donald J. "Leisure Time Activities in Bangor, 1865–1901." MA, History, University of Maine, 1961.

ABOUT THE AUTHOR

Wayne E. Reilly worked for the *Bangor Daily News* for twenty-eight years as a reporter, editorial writer and assignment editor. After retiring, he began indulging his love of history by writing a weekly column for the newspaper about life in Bangor a century ago. During the last ten years, he has written hundreds of columns based on events found in the city's century-old newspapers. Reilly has written many freelance stories for *Down East*, *Maine Times* and other publications. He has won many professional and civic awards for his reporting, writing and editing during his career. He has an AB degree in English from Bowdoin College and an MA in journalism from the University of Missouri. A previous book of his newspaper history columns, *Remembering Bangor: The Queen City Before the Great Fire*, was published in 2009 by The History Press. He has also edited two Civil War books based on family diaries and letters: *Sarah Jane Foster: Teacher of the Freedmen* and *The Diaries of Sarah Jane and Emma Ann Foster: A Year in Maine During the Civil War*.

Visit us at
www.historypress.net

www.ingramcontent.com/pod-product-compliance
Lightning Source LLC
Chambersburg PA
CBHW060802100426
42813CB00004B/917